INTELLIGENCE AND SECURITY INFORMATICS FOR INTERNATIONAL SECURITY

INTEGRATED SERIES IN INFORMATION SYSTEMS

Series Editors

Professor Ramesh Sharda
Oklahoma State University

Prof. Dr. Stefan Voß
Universität Hamburg

Other published titles in the series:

INTELLIGENCE AND SECURITY INFORMATICS FOR INTERNATIONAL SECURITY

Information Sharing and Data Mining

Hsinchun Chen, Ph.D.

McClelland Professor of MIS
Director, Artificial Intelligence Lab and
Director, NSF COPLINK Center
Management Information Systems Department
Eller College of Management, University of Arizona

 Springer

Hsinchun Chen
The University of Arizona, USA

ISBN-10: 0-387-30332-4 (e-book)
ISBN: 978-1-4419-3733-9   ISBN-13: 978-0387-30332-1 (e-book)

9 8 7 6 5 4 3 2 1

springer.com

DEDICATION

I dedicate this book, with love, to the memory of my father, Kuang-Shen Chen (1933-1997) and my brother, I-Chun (Jingo) Chen (1961-2000). This book also owes much to support from my family, in particular, my mom, Fu-Lien; my wife, Hsiao-Hui (Sherry); and my daughter and son, Hillary and Hugh. I would also like to thank the funding agencies, research partners, and all my mentors, colleagues, and students for their wisdom, encouragement, and inspiration over the years. Last but not least, I would like to thank Cathy Larson, Danitza Garcia, and Gary Folven for making the book production process professional and easy (for me).

As a graduate student at New York University (NYU) from 1985 to 1989, I spent many hours working on the NYU Wall Street and Washington Square campuses and taking the late-night subway trains from the World Trade Center to Queens and then to New Jersey. My heart ached on the day of September 11, 2001, and long after. May the heroes and citizens who perished in this tragic event rest in peace; and may the world never see another tragedy like this again.

TABLE OF CONTENTS

x

PREFACE

The commitment of the scientific, engineering, and health communities to helping the U.S. and the world respond to security challenges became evident after September 11, 2001. The U.S. National Research Council's report on "Making the Nation Safer: The Role of Science and Technology in Countering Terrorism" recommends that "a strategic long-term research and development agenda should be established to address three primary counterterrorism-related areas in IT: information and network security, the IT needs of emergency responders, and information fusion and management."

In order to address these pressing and challenging national security research and development needs, many federal government and policy agencies, intelligence and public safety community, defense contractors, IT companies, national laboratories, and various academic research centers and institutions have begun to engage in significant Research & Development activities in national security. A new science of "Intelligence and Security Informatics" (ISI), akin to biomedical informatics, has begun to emerge and will continue to influence a new generation of policy makers, practitioners, researchers, and students.

The R&D in information and network security should include approaches and architectures for prevention, identification, and containment of cyber-intrusions and recovery from them. The R&D to address IT needs of emergency responders should include ensuring interoperability, maintaining and expanding communications capability during an emergency, communicating with the public during an emergency, and providing support for decision makers. The R&D in information fusion and management for the intelligence, law enforcement, and emergency response communities should include data mining, data integration, language technologies, and processing of image and audio data.

This monograph is based on nearly a decade of cutting-edge and hands-on law enforcement, intelligence, and security informatics research and community building experience of Dr. Hsinchun Chen and his lab/center – the Artificial Intelligence Lab and the NSF COPLINK Center for Intelligence and Security Research. The monograph presents a national security research framework and discusses related IT technical components, directions, and past research, especially focusing on information sharing and data mining. Drawing from our own research experience, the book also includes many detailed case studies of how such technologies are developed and adopted in critical law enforcement, emergency response, intelligence analysis, and terrorism research contexts. This monograph expands significantly from an earlier review article in *Annual Review of Information Science and Technology (ARIST)*, Volume 40, 2005 (Chen and Xu, 2005).

SCOPE AND ORGANIZATION

The monograph aims to present its chapters in a manner understandable and useful to students, researchers, and security professionals. The first four chapters provide an overview of the field, including discussions of research challenges, an ISI research framework, literature review of the field, and national security critical mission areas. Seventeen case studies based on our previous and ongoing research are then provided in six subsequent chapters (corresponding to six national security critical mission areas) to allow readers to get a closer look at the implementation challenges and opportunities. Chapter 11 presents important considerations for forming research partnerships in national security. The final chapter provides conclusions and future directions. In each chapter, we summarize future research opportunities and present questions for discussion in classes or seminars. The book also includes samples of a user data license and Memorandum of Understanding, and more than 150 references to research of relevance to homeland security research. The titles of the twelve chapters are listed below:

- Chapter 1. Intelligence and Security Informatics (ISI): Challenges and Opportunities
- Chapter 2. An Information Sharing and Data Mining Research Framework
- Chapter 3. ISI Research: Literature Review
- Chapter 4. National Security Critical Mission Areas and Case Studies
- Chapter 5. Intelligence and Warning
- Chapter 6. Border and Transportation Security
- Chapter 7. Domestic Counter-terrorism
- Chapter 8. Protecting Critical Infrastructure and Key Assets
- Chapter 9. Defending Against Catastrophic Terrorism
- Chapter 10. Emergency Preparedness and Responses
- Chapter 11. The Partnership and Collaboration Framework
- Chapter 12. Conclusions and Future Directions

AUDIENCE

The primary audience for the monograph includes the following:

- College professors, research scientists, graduate students, and select undergraduate juniors and seniors in computer science, information management, information science, and other related public safety, intelligence analysis, and terrorism research disciplines;

- Researchers, analysts, and policy makers in federal departments, national laboratories, intelligence community, public safety and law enforcement agencies, and the emergency response community;

- Consultants and practitioners in IT hardware, communication, and software companies, consulting firms, and defense contractors.

We hope the readers will find the monograph of value to them. We also hope that future ISI research will continue to help improve information sharing among national security agencies and increase collaboration among academics, local, state, and federal agencies, and industry, thereby bringing positive contributions to all aspects of our society.

Hsinchun Chen
University of Arizona

AUTHOR BIOGRAPHY

Dr. Hsinchun Chen is McClelland Professor of Management Information Systems (4th ranked by the US News and World Report for 15+ years) at the University of Arizona and Andersen Consulting Professor of the Year (1999). He received the B.S. degree from the National Chiao-Tung University in Taiwan, the MBA degree from the State University of New York (SUNY) at Buffalo, and the Ph.D. degree in Information Systems from the New York University. He is the author of nine books and more than 200 articles covering intelligence analysis, data/text/web mining, digital libraries, knowledge management, medical informatics, and Web computing. His two recent books include: "Medical Informatics: Knowledge Management and Data Mining in Biomedicine" and "Intelligence and Security Informatics: Information Sharing and Data Mining," both published by Springer.

He serves on the editorial board of *ACM Transactions on Information Systems;IEEE Transactions on Intelligent Transportation Systems; IEEE Transactions on Systems, Man, and Cybernetics; Journal of the American Society for Information Science and Technology;* and *Decision Support Systems.* Dr. Chen is a Scientific Counselor/Advisor of the National Library of Medicine (U.S.A.), Academia Sinica (Taiwan), and the National Library of China (China), and has served as an advisor for major NSF, DOJ, NLM, and other international research programs in digital library, digital government, medical informatics, and national security research. He is a member of the Board of Governors of the IEEE Intelligent Transportation Systems Society and the technical committee chair in homeland security.

Dr. Chen is the founding director of the Artificial Intelligence Lab and the Hoffman E-Commerce Lab. The UA Artificial Intelligence Lab, which houses 40+ researchers, has received more than $20M in research funding from NSF, NIH, NLM, DOJ, CIA, and other agencies over the past 15 years. The Hoffman E-Commerce Lab, which has been funded primarily through major IT industry partners, is equipped with supercomputing power, enterprise-scale e-commerce applications, and terabyte storage, and places the Eller College and the UA MIS Department among the most IT-savvy institutions in the country.

Dr. Chen served as conference co-chair of ACM/IEEE Joint Conference on Digital Libraries (JCDL) in 2004 and has served as the steering committee chair for the past seven International Conferences of Asian Digital Libraries (ICADL), 1998-2004 (which he founded in 1997). Dr. Chen is also a pioneer in Intelligence and Security Informatics research. He has served as conference co-chair of the IEEE International Conferences on Intelligence and Security Informatics (ISI) 2003, 2004, and 2005. The ISI conference, which has been sponsored by NSF, CIA, DHS, and NIJ, has become the premiere meeting for national and homeland security IT research.

Dr. Chen's COPLINK system, which has been quoted as a national model for public safety information sharing and analysis, has been adopted in more than 100 law enforcement and intelligence agencies. COPLINK research, which includes significant innovations in information integration, criminal network analysis, deception detection, and spatial-temporal visualization, had been featured in the *New York Times*, *Newsweek*, *Los Angeles Times*, *Washington Post*, and *Boston Globe*, among others. The COPLINK project was selected as a finalist by the prestigious International Association of Chiefs of Police (IACP)/Motorola 2003 Weaver Seavey Award for Quality in Law Enforcement in 2003. COPLINK research has been expanded recently to include border protection (BorderSafe), disease and bioagent surveillance (BioPortal), and terrorism informatics research (Dark Web), with additional funding provided by NSF, CIA, and DHS.

Dr. Chen has also received numerous industry awards in information technology and knowledge management education and research including: AT&T Foundation Award, SAP Award, the Andersen Consulting Professor of the Year Award, and the University of Arizona Technology Innovation Award. He also received the Distinguished Alumnus Award from the National Chiao-Tung University in Taiwan.

Photograph of Dr. Hsinchun Chen

Photograph of members of the Artificial Intelligence Lab, with family and friends at the annual Artificial Intelligence Lab Picnic, 2005

Chapter 1

INTELLIGENCE AND SECURITY INFORMATICS (ISI): CHALLENGES AND OPPORTUNITIES

Chapter Overview

The tragic events of September 11th and the following anthrax contamination of letters caused drastic effects on many aspects of society. Academics in the fields of natural sciences, computational science, information science, social sciences, engineering, medicine, and many others have been called upon to help enhance the government's ability to fight terrorism and other crimes. Six critical mission areas have been identified where information technology can contribute, as suggested in the "National Strategy for Homeland Security" report, including: *intelligence and warning, border and transportation security, domestic counter-terrorism, protecting critical infrastructure, defending against catastrophic terrorism,* and *emergency preparedness and responses.* Facing the critical missions of national security and various data and technical challenges, we believe there is a pressing need to develop the science of "Intelligence and Security Informatics" (ISI). This chapter reviews ISI research challenges, compares ISI with the development of Biomedical Informatics, and suggests federal funding initiatives and research opportunities of relevance to ISI.

1.1   Introduction

The tragic events of September 11th and the following anthrax contamination of letters caused drastic effects on many aspects of society. Terrorism became the most significant threat to national security because of its potential to bring massive damage to our infrastructure, economy, and people.

In response to this challenge, federal authorities are actively implementing comprehensive strategies and measures in order to achieve the three objectives identified in the "National Strategy for Homeland Security" report (Office of Homeland Security, 2002): (1) preventing future terrorist attacks, (2) reducing the nation's vulnerability, and (3) minimizing the damage and recovering from attacks that occur. State and local law enforcement agencies, likewise, are becoming more vigilant about the criminal activities that harm public safety and threaten national security.

Academics in the fields of natural sciences, computational science, information science, social sciences, engineering, medicine, and many others have been called upon to help enhance the government's ability to fight terrorism and other crimes. Science and technology have been identified in the "National Strategy for Homeland Security" report as the keys to win the new counter-terrorism war (Office of Homeland Security, 2002). It is widely believed that information technology will play an indispensable role in making our nation safer (National Research Council, 2002) by supporting intelligence and knowledge discovery through collecting, processing, analyzing, and utilizing terrorism- and crime-related data (Chen et al., 2003a; Chen et al., 2004b). Based on the crime and intelligence knowledge discovered, the federal, state, and local authorities can make timely decisions to select effective strategies and tactics as well as allocate the appropriate amount of resources to detect, prevent, and respond to future attacks.

1.2   Information Technology and National Security

Six critical mission areas have been identified where information technology can contribute to the accomplishment of the three strategic national security objectives identified in the "National Strategy for Homeland Security" report (Office of Homeland Security, 2002):

- *Intelligence and Warning.* Although terrorism depends on surprise to damage its targets (Office of Homeland Security, 2002), terrorist activities are not random and impossible to track. Terrorists must plan and prepare before the execution of an attack by selecting a target, recruiting and training executors, acquiring financial support, and traveling to the country where the target is located (Sageman, 2004). To avoid being preempted by authorities they may hide their true identities and disguise attack-related activities. Similarly, criminals may use falsified identities during police contacts (Wang et al., 2004a). Although it is difficult, detecting potential terrorist attacks or crimes is possible and feasible with the help of information technology. By analyzing the communication and activity patterns among terrorists and their contacts (i.e., terrorist networks), detecting deceptive identities, or employing other surveillance and monitoring techniques, intelligence and warning systems may issue timely, critical alerts and warnings to prevent attacks or crimes from occurring.

- *Border and Transportation Security.* Terrorists enter a targeted country through an air, land, or sea port of entry. Criminals in narcotics rings travel across borders to purchase, carry, distribute, and sell drugs. Information, such as travelers' identities, images, fingerprints, vehicles used, and other characteristics, is collected from customs, borders, and immigration authorities on a daily basis. Counter-terrorism and crime-fighting capabilities can be greatly improved by the creation of a "smart border," where information from multiple sources is shared and analyzed to help locate wanted terrorists or criminals. Technologies such as information sharing and integration, collaboration and communication, biometrics, and image and speech recognition will be greatly needed in such smart borders.

- *Domestic Counter-terrorism.* As terrorists, both international and domestic, may be involved in local crimes, state and local law enforcement agencies are also contributing to the missions by investigating and prosecuting crimes. Terrorism, like gangs and narcotics trafficking, is regarded as a type of organized crime in which multiple offenders cooperate to carry out offenses. Information technologies that help find cooperative relationships between criminals and their interactive patterns would also be helpful for analyzing terrorism. Monitoring activities of domestic terrorist and extremist groups using advanced information technologies will also be helpful to public safety personnel and policy makers.

- *Protecting Critical Infrastructure and Key Assets.* Roads, bridges, water supplies, and many other physical service systems are critical infrastructure and key assets of a nation. They may become the target of terrorist attacks because of their vulnerabilities (Office of Homeland Security, 2002). Moreover, virtual (cyber) infrastructure such as the Internet may also be vulnerable to intrusions and inside threats (Lee and

Stolfo, 1998). Criminals and terrorists are increasingly using cyberspace to conduct illegal activities, share ideology, solicit funding, and recruit. In addition to physical devices such as sensors and detectors, advanced information technologies are needed to model the normal behaviors of the usage of these systems and then use the models to distinguish abnormal behaviors from normal behaviors. Protective or reactive measures can be selected based on the results to secure these assets from attacks.

- *Defending Against Catastrophic Terrorism.* Terrorist attacks can cause devastating damage to a society through the use of chemical, biological, or radiological weapons. Biological attacks, for example, may cause contamination, infectious disease outbreaks, and significant loss of life. Information systems that can efficiently and effectively collect, access, analyze, and report data about catastrophe-leading events can help prevent, detect, respond to, and manage these attacks (Damianos et al., 2002).

- *Emergency Preparedness and Responses.* In case of a national emergency, prompt and effective responses are critical to reduce the damage resulting from an attack. In addition to the systems that are prepared to defend against catastrophes, information technologies that help design and experiment with optimized response plans (Lu et al., 2003), identify experts, train response professionals, and manage consequences are beneficial in the long run. Moreover, information systems that facilitate social and psychological support to the victims of terrorist attacks can also help society recover from disasters.

Although it is important for the critical missions of national security, the development of information technology for counter-terrorism and crime-fighting applications faces many problems and challenges.

1.3   Problems and Challenges

Currently, intelligence and security agencies are gathering large amounts of data from various sources. Processing and analyzing such data, however, has become increasingly difficult. By treating terrorism as a form of organized crime, these challenges can be categorized into three types:

- *Characteristics of criminals and crimes.* Some crimes may be geographically diffused and temporally dispersed. In organized crimes such as transnational narcotics trafficking, criminals often live in different countries, states, and cities. Drug distribution and sales occur in different places at different times. Similar situations exist in other organized crimes (e.g., terrorism, armed robbery, and gang-related crime). As a result, an investigation must cover multiple offenders who commit criminal activities in different places at different times. This can be fairly difficult given the limited resources that intelligence and security agencies have. Moreover, as computer and Internet technologies advance, criminals are utilizing cyberspace to commit various types of cybercrimes under the disguise of ordinary online transactions and communications.

- *Characteristics of crime and intelligence related data.* A significant source of challenge is information stovepipe and overload resulting from diverse data sources, multiple data formats, and large data volumes. Unlike other domains such as marketing, finance, and medicine in which data can be collected from particular sources (e.g., sales records from companies, patient medical history from hospitals), the intelligence and security domain does not have a well-defined data source. Both authoritative information (e.g., crime incident reports, telephone records, financial statements, immigration and customs records) and open source information (e.g., news stories, journal articles, books, web pages) need to be gathered for investigative purposes. Data collected from these different sources often are in different formats ranging from structured database records to unstructured text, image, audio, and video files. Important information such as criminal associations may be available but contained in unstructured, multilingual texts and remains difficult to access and retrieve. Moreover, as data volumes continue to grow, extracting valuable and credible intelligence and knowledge becomes a difficult problem.

- *Characteristics of crime and intelligence analysis techniques.* Current research on the technologies for counter-terrorism and crime-fighting applications lacks a consistent framework addressing the major challenges. Some information technologies including data integration, data analysis, text mining, image and video processing, and evidence combination have been identified as being particularly helpful (National Research Council, 2002). However, the question of how to employ them in the intelligence and security domain and use them to effectively address the critical mission areas of national security remains unanswered.

Facing the critical missions of national security and various data and technical challenges, we believe there is a pressing need to develop the science of "Intelligence and Security Informatics" (ISI) (Chen et al., 2003a; Chen et al., 2004b), with its main objective being the "development of advanced information technologies, systems, algorithms, and databases for national security-related applications, through an integrated technological, organizational, and policy-based approach" (Chen et al., 2003a).

1.4 Intelligence and Security Informatics vs. Biomedical Informatics: Emergence of a Discipline

Comparing ISI with Biomedical Informatics, an established academic discipline addressing information management issues in biological and medical applications (Shortliffe and Blois, 2000; Chen et al., 2005), we found tremendous analogies between these two disciplines. Table 1-1 summarizes the similarities and differences between ISI and Biomedical Informatics.

Table 1-1. Analogies between ISI and Biomedical Informatics.

		Biomedical Informatics	ISI
Challenges	Domain-specific	• Complexity and uncertainty associated with organisms and diseases • Critical decisions regarding patient well-being and biomedical discoveries	• Geographically diffused and temporally dispersed organized crimes • Cyber-crimes on the Internet • Critical decisions related to public safety and homeland security
	Data	• Information stovepipe and overload • HL7 XML standard • PHIN MS messaging • Patient records, diseases data, medical images	• Information stovepipe and overload • Justice XML standard • Criminal incident records • Multilingual intelligence open sources
	Technology	• Ontologies and linguistic parsing • Information integration • Data and text mining • Medical decision-support systems and techniques	• Information integration • Criminal network analysis • Data, text, and web mining • Identity management and deception detection
	Methodology	KDD	KDD
Contributions	Scientific	• Computer and information science, sociology, policy, legal • Clinical medicine and biology	• Computer and information science, sociology, policy, legal • Criminology, terrorism research
	Practical	• Public health • Patient well-being • Biomedical treatment and discovery	• Crime investigation and counter-terrorism • National and homeland security

In terms of data characteristics, they both face the information stovepipe and information overload problem. In terms of technology development, they both are searching for new approaches, methods, and innovative use of existing techniques. In terms of scientific contributions, they both may add new insights and knowledge to various academic disciplines.

Most importantly, as a consistent research framework based on knowledge management and data mining has begun to emerge in biomedical informatics (Chen et al., 2005), ISI also needs a framework to guide its research. Facing the unique challenges (and associated opportunities) of information overload and the pressing need for advanced criminal and intelligence analyses and investigations, we believe that the Knowledge Discovery from Databases (KDD) methodology (Fayyad and Uthurusamy, 2002), which has achieved significant success in other information-intensive, knowledge-critical domains including business, engineering, biology, and medicine, could be critical in addressing the challenges and problems facing ISI. More details about such a research framework will be discussed in the following chapter.

1.5   Federal Initiatives and Funding Opportunities in ISI

Similar to biocomputing and biomedical informatics, a new, emerging, and critical discipline such as ISI not only can spark the imagination and excitement of society, but it also draws the attention of federal funding agencies. As a testament to the importance of ISI-related research, the United States National Science Foundation (NSF) publicly stated its strong commitment to national security research (as stipulated in its founding mandate), in addition to its traditional leadership role in basic science and engineering research and education. Many federal research and funding agencies in the United States have established new research programs that aim to address different facets of national security research.Without intending to be comprehensive, we summarize some significant past and ongoing federal funding programs of relevance to ISI, especially for academic researchers in universities and research institutes. There is much information about national security-related funding opportunities for commercial companies and vendors which will not be covered in this chapter.

- National Science Foundation (NSF): The NSF has issued several Information Technology Research (ITR) program announcements with a national security focus. The computing (CISE) and behavioral (SBE) divisions of NSF are encouraging multi-disciplinary research projects of relevance to ISI. The NSF/CIA KDD (Knowledge Discovery and

Dissemination) program is a good example of joint NSF and intelligence community funding initiatives. Most of the NSF-funded projects stress scientific innovation.

- Department of Homeland Security (DHS): DHS probably has the largest number of research initiatives of relevance to ISI due to its agency mission. Four university-based homeland security research centers have been established. Many new ad hoc initiatives such as terrorism informatics research, bioagent surveillance, smart border, biometrics, deception detection, and critical infrastructure protection are also under active development. DHS-funded projects tend to be more problem-specific. Due to a lack of staff support, personnel turnover, and inexperience in funded research, the DHS proposal review process is significantly less structured than that of NSF.

- Department of Defense (DOD) and Intelligence Community: After the disastrous ending of the TIA (Total Information Awareness) program spearheaded by former Admiral Poindexter, the DOD and the intelligence community have not publicized many new research activities of relevance to ISI. One exception may be the ARDA (Advanced Research & Development Activity) program that aims to develop advanced information technologies for the intelligence community. The abovementioned joint NSF/CIA KDD program that draws top-notch researchers to perform unclassified national security and intelligence research is an excellent model for advanced and potentially high-impact ISI research.

- Center for Disease Control and Prevention (CDC) and National Institutes of Health (NIH): Not surprisingly, CDC and NIH are supporting national security research of relevance to infectious diseases and bioagent surveillance. The National Library of Medicine has issued solicitations in crisis management of relevance to public health. Similar to DHS, CDC appropriates significant funding to state and local jurisdictions for their public health, disease surveillance, and emergency response needs. Although such projects are often short-term and implementation-oriented in nature, university researchers can benefit from collaborating with state and local public health agencies, and vice versa.

- Department of Justice (DOJ): DOJ and its research arm, National Institute of Justice (NIJ), traditionally fund research and development projects of relevance to local and state public safety and law enforcement agencies. Due to the importance of domestic counter-terrorism, focused counter-terrorism research programs have been developed at NIJ. Most of the NIJ projects are of smaller scale and single-PI in nature due to the agency's limited funding ability. Most projects need to demonstrate significant public-safety relevance and value.

- Office of Naval Research (ONR), Air Force Research Labs, private foundations, and others: There are many other funding opportunities with other traditional armed forces-specific federal funding agencies. Most of them have either adjusted or are adjusting their existing research programs to be of relevance to the new homeland security mission. Several private foundations have also begun to support selected homeland security-related research, in particular, in citizen responses, disaster relief, and education.

For our readers we include a listing of sample federal program announcements of relevance to ISI in the section below. The list is not intended to be comprehensive, but to illustrate the abundant research and funding opportunities in ISI. Readers are advised to perform periodic searches on the web for ongoing program announcements.

- National Science Foundation (NSF), Information Technology Research (ITR) Program: The NSF ITR Program has been successful in opening up opportunities at the frontiers of IT research and education. In its fourth year, FY 2003, the program stimulated research on the fundamental challenges facing the continued expansion and utilization of IT across the sciences and engineering, the creation of novel uses of IT, the interaction of IT with society at large, and the use of IT to enhance security and reduce society's vulnerabilities to catastrophic events, whether natural or man-made. In FY 2004, the focus is "ITR for National Priorities." Particular emphasis is placed on the distributed systems, grids and infrastructures that support the attainment of these national priorities.

- Department of Homeland Security (DHS): Through the Homeland Security Centers of Excellence Program, DHS is investing in university-based partnerships to develop centers of multi-disciplinary research where important fields of inquiry can be analyzed and best practices developed, debated, and shared. DHS selected the University of Southern California to house the first HS-Center, known as the Homeland Security Center for Risk and Economic Analysis of Terrorism Events (CREATE). Texas A&M University and its partners were selected as the HS-Center for Foreign Animal and Zoonotic Disease Defense. The University of Minnesota and its partners were selected as the HS-Center for Food Protection and Defense, which will address agro-security issues related to post-harvest food protection. The University of Maryland's team and its partners were selected recently as the fourth HS-center to study the social, economic, and psychological dimensions of terrorism research.

The DHS Innovative Architectures for Unified Incident Command and Decision Support Program seeks proposals for an innovative information management and sharing architecture that answers the growing needs of the emergency responder community. This solicitation seeks to confront the technical challenges associated with the development of such innovative, modular, scaleable, and secure information management architecture.

The DHS Security Research and Development Program seeks the development and deployment of technologies to protect the nation's cyber infrastructure, including the Internet and other critical infrastructures that depend on computer systems for their mission.

- National Institutes of Health (NIH), National Library of Medicine (NLM), Informatics for Disaster Management Program: The National Library of Medicine, the National Institute of Mental Health, and the National Institute of Biomedical Imaging and Bioengineering support informatics research that addresses biomedical information management problems relevant to management of disasters. Disasters can be caused by nature or by man, through accident or by malice. Terrorism, particularly bioterrorism, is now an important focus of federal activity, but terrorism is only one of a number of threats to public safety classified as disasters. Disaster management is heavily dependent on efficient flow of information. How best to utilize information technology in a disaster situation poses a number of problems for which relevant informatics research is necessary.

- Center for Disease Control and Prevention (CDC), National Center for Infectious Diseases (NCID), Bioterrorism Extramural Research Grant Program: The main functions of the CDC NCID Office include: program coordination, surveillance integration and informatics activities, and analytical activities of relevance to infectious diseases. The NCID Office of Extramural Research funded $8.4 million dollars for nine biodefense research grants in FY03. The NCID areas of interest for bioterrorism and infectious disease research include: surveillance and epidemiology, interruption of transmission, and environmental detection.

- Department of Defense (DOD), Advanced Research and Development Activity (ARDA) Program: The Advanced Research and Development Activity (ARDA) program is an Intelligence Community (IC) center for conducting advanced research and development related to information technology (IT) (information stored, transmitted, or manipulated by electronic means). ARDA sponsors high risk, high payoff research designed to produce new technology to address some of the most important and challenging IT problems faced by the intelligence community. The research is currently organized into five technology thrusts: Information Exploitation, Quantum Information Science, Global Infosystems Access, Novel Intelligence from Massive Data, and Advanced Information Assurance. Recent solicitations include: Advanced Question and Answering for Intelligence; Video Analysis and Content Extraction (VACE) Phase II; Proactive and Predictive Information Assurance for Next Geneva Systems; Advanced Countermeasures for Insider Threat; Information Assurance for the U.S. Intelligence Community; and Advanced Question and Answering Phase I.

- Department of Justice (DOJ), National Institute of Justice (NIJ): The National Institute of Justice (NIJ) is the research, development, and evaluation agency of the U.S. Department of Justice and a component of the Office of Justice Programs. NIJ provides objective, independent, evidence-based knowledge and tools to enhance the administration of justice and public safety.

The NIJ's Situational Aspects of Crime Program seeks research that examines situational characteristics and the events that lead up to criminal acts in order to identify target points for prevention and intervention. Research under this solicitation should focus on the characteristics of criminal events or the interactions between the characteristics of situations and individuals.

Their Terrorism and Transnational Crime Program seeks research and evaluation that will inform national policy and practice related to terrorism, transnational criminal behavior, and any connections between them. Proposed research should aim to improve criminal justice and first responder strategies for prevention of, preparation for, response to, and mitigation of terrorist incidents at the federal, state, and local levels.

1.6   Future Directions

The emergence of a new discipline such as ISI would require careful cultivation and development by many top-notch researchers and practitioners from many different disciplines, including (but not limited to): computer science, information science, information systems, electrical engineering, social science, law, public policy, criminal justice, terrorism research, psychology, behavioral and economic sciences, management science, bioinformatics, public health, etc. There is an abundance of opportunities for developing new and innovative funded ISI-related projects.

Regardless of which funding programs you may be considering for your research, there are some common characteristics among successfully funded and (eventually, after execution) high-impact projects:

- Unique and critical scientific or engineering innovations: You need to clearly distinguish your research from others.

- Important problems and significant partners: You need to address important national security problems and demonstrate your commitment to address these problems with the help and support of your local, state, and federal agency partners.

- From small to large: Most funded projects began humbly with proof-of-concept level funding.

- A multi-disciplinary team: After initial success, a multi-disciplinary team of computer scientists, system developers, social scientists, policy and legal experts, domain (intelligence and security) experts, and such will be needed to implement a full-scale, multi-phased, complex national security-related project.

- Aim high: The following tangible (but somewhat lofty) project goals are always good for your project team to aim at: (1) publishing your project findings in *Science, Nature*, or *Proceedings of the Academy of Science* (for its scientific contributions); and (2) being featured in a *New York Times* or *USA Today* front page article (for its societal impact).

1.7 Questions for Discussion

1. What are some ways to identify potentially relevant federal funding programs? How can the topics to focus on be determined? How do you interact with relevant program managers and directors for feedback? How do you get invited to a PI-only meeting when you are not a PI yet (but would like to become a PI)? How frequently do you need to travel to DC for project meetings?

2. What are some ways to identify critical local, state, and federal partners for your research project? How do you convince them of your value? How do you get their letters of support, data, and commitment of time and personnel? How can you make the system work for all involved?

3. What are some ways to publish your work in this area? Which conferences and journals would be best? How can you publicize your work with the media and the press?

Chapter 2

AN ISI RESEARCH FRAMEWORK: INFORMATION SHARING AND DATA MINING

Chapter Overview

To address the data and technical challenges facing ISI, we present a research framework with a primary focus on KDD (Knowledge Discovery from Databases) technologies. The framework is discussed in the context of crime types and security implications. Selected data mining techniques, including information sharing and collaboration, association mining, classification and clustering, text mining, spatial and temporal mining, and criminal network analysis, are believed to be critical to criminal and intelligence analyses and investigations. In addition to the technical discussions, the chapter also discusses caveats for data mining and important civil liberties considerations.

2.1 Introduction

Crime is an act or the commission of an act that is forbidden, or the omission of a duty that is commanded by a public law and that makes the offender liable to punishment by that law. The more threat a crime type poses on public safety, the more likely it is to be of national security concern. Some crimes such as traffic violations, theft, and homicide are mainly in the jurisdiction of local law enforcement agencies. Some other crimes need to be dealt with by both local law enforcement and national security authorities. Identity theft and fraud, for instance, are relevant at both the local and national level -- criminals may escape arrest by using false identities; drug smugglers may enter the United States by holding counterfeited passports or visas. Organized crimes, such as terrorism and narcotics trafficking, are often diffuse geographically, resulting in common security concerns across cities, states, and countries. Cybercrimes can pose threats to public safety across multiple jurisdictional areas due to the widespread nature of computer networks.

Table 2-1 summarizes the different types of crimes sorted by the degree of their respective public influence (Chen et al., 2004a). International and domestic terrorism, in particular, often involves multiple crime types (e.g., identity theft, money laundering, arson and bombing, organized and violent activities, and cyber-terrorism) and causes great damage.

2.2 An ISI Research Framework

We believe that KDD techniques can play a central role in improving counter-terrorism and crime-fighting capabilities of intelligence, security, and law enforcement agencies by reducing the cognitive and information overload. Knowledge discovery refers to non-trivial extraction of implicit, previously unknown, and potentially useful knowledge from data. Knowledge discovery techniques promise easy, convenient, and practical exploration of very large collections of data for organizations and users, and have been applied in marketing, finance, manufacturing, biology, and many other domains (e.g., predicting consumer behaviors, detecting credit card frauds, or clustering genes that have similar biological functions) (Fayyad and Uthurusamy, 2002). Traditional knowledge discovery techniques include association rules mining, classification and prediction, cluster analysis, and outlier analysis (Han and Kamber, 2001). As natural language processing (NLP) research advances, text mining approaches that automatically extract, summarize, categorize, and translate text documents have also been widely used (Chen, 2001; Trybula, 1999).

Many of these KDD technologies could be applied in ISI studies (Chen et al., 2003a; Chen et al., 2004b). Keeping in mind the special characteristics of crimes, criminals, and crime-related data, we categorize existing ISI technologies into six classes: *information sharing and collaboration, crime association mining, crime classification and clustering, intelligence text mining, spatial and temporal crime mining,* and *criminal network mining.*

Table 2-1. Crime types and security concerns.

Crime Type	Local Law Enforcement Level	National Security Level
Traffic Violations	Driving under influence (DUI), fatal/personal injury/property damage, traffic accident, road rage	-
Sex Crime	Sexual offenses, sexual assaults, child molesting	Organized prostitution, people smuggling
Theft	Robbery, burglary, larceny, motor vehicle theft, stolen property	Theft of national secrets or weapon information
Fraud	Forgery and counterfeiting, fraud, embezzlement, identity deception	Transnational money laundering, identity fraud, transnational financial fraud
Arson	Arson on buildings, apartments	-
Organized Crime	Narcotic drug offenses (sales or possession), gang-related offenses,	Transnational drug trafficking, terrorism (bioterrorism, bombing, hijacking, etc.)
Violent Crime	Criminal homicide, armed robbery, aggravated assault, other assaults	Terrorism
Cyber Crime	Internet fraud (e.g., credit card fraud, advance fee fraud, fraudulent web sites), illegal trading, network intrusion/hacking, virus spreading, hate crimes, cyber-piracy, cyber-pornography, cyber-terrorism, theft of confidential information	

(Vertical axis label: Increasing Public Influence)

These six classes are grounded on traditional knowledge discovery technologies with a few new approaches added, including spatial and temporal crime pattern mining and criminal network analysis, which are more relevant to counter-terrorism and crime investigation. Although information sharing and collaboration are not data mining *per se*, they help prepare, normalize, warehouse, and integrate data for knowledge discovery and thus are included in the framework.

In Figure 2-1 we present our proposed research framework, with the horizontal axis being the crimes types and the vertical axis being the six classes of techniques (Chen et al., 2004a). The shaded regions on the chart show promising research areas, i.e., that a certain class of techniques is relevant to solving a certain type of crime. Note that more serious crimes may require a more complete set of knowledge discovery techniques. For example, the investigation of organized crimes such as terrorism may depend on criminal network analysis technology, which requires the use of other knowledge discovery techniques such as association mining and clustering. An important observation about this framework is that the high-frequency occurrences and strong association patterns of severe and organized crimes such as terrorism and narcotics present a unique opportunity and potentially high rewards for adopting such a knowledge discovery framework.

Several unique classes of data mining techniques are of great relevance to ISI research. *Text mining* is critical for extracting key entities (people, places, narcotics, weapons, time, etc.) and their relationships presented in voluminous police incident reports, intelligence reports, open source news clips, etc. Some of these techniques need to be multilingual in nature, including the abilities for machine translation and cross-lingual information retrieval (CLIR). *Spatial and temporal mining and visualization* are often needed for geographic information systems (GIS) and temporal analysis of criminal and terrorist events. Most crime analysts are well trained in GIS-based crime mapping tools; however, automated spatial and temporal pattern mining techniques (e.g., hotspot analysis) have not been adopted widely in intelligence and security applications.

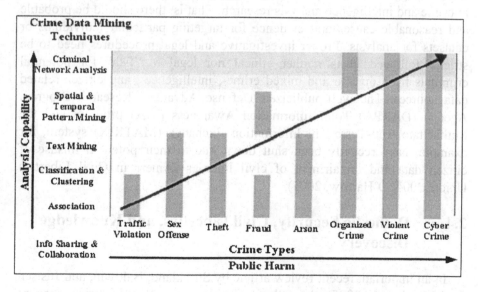

Figure 2-1. A knowledge discovery research framework for ISI.

Organized criminals (e.g., gangs and narcotics) and terrorists often form inter-connected covert networks for their illegal activities. Often referred to as "dark networks," these organizations exhibit unique structures, communication channels, and resilience to attack and disruption. New computational techniques, including social network analysis, network learning, and network topological analysis (e.g., random network, small-world network, and scale-free network), are needed for the systematic study of those complex and covert networks. We broadly consider these techniques under *criminal network analysis* in Figure 2-1.

2.3 Caveats for Data Mining

Before we review in detail relevant ISI-related data mining techniques, applications, and literature in the next chapter, we wish to briefly discuss the legal and ethical caveats regarding crime and intelligence research.

The potential negative effects of intelligence gathering and analysis on the privacy and civil liberties of the public have been well publicized (Cook and Cook, 2003). There exist many laws, regulations, and agreements governing data collection, confidentiality, and reporting, which could directly impact the development and application of ISI technologies. We strongly recommend that intelligence and security agencies and ISI researchers be aware of these laws and regulations in research. Moreover, we also suggest that a hypothesis-guided, evidence-based approach be used in crime and intelligence analysis research. That is, there should be probable and reasonable causes and evidence for targeting particular individuals or datasets for analysis. Proper investigative and legal procedures need to be strictly followed. It is neither ethical nor legal to "fish" for potential criminals from diverse and mixed crime-, intelligence-, and citizen-related data sources. The well-publicized Defense Advanced Research Program Agency (DARPA) Total Information Awareness (TIA) program and the Multi-State Anti-Terrorism Information Exchange (MATRIX) system, for example, have recently been shut down due to their potential misuse of citizen data and impairment of civil liberties (American Civil Liberties Union, 2004; O'Harrow, 2005).

2.4 Domestic Security, Civil Liberties, and Knowledge Discovery

In an important recent review article by Strickland, Baldwin, and Justsen (Strickland et al., 2005), the authors provide an excellent historical account of government surveillance in the United States. The article presents new surveillance initiatives in the age of terrorism (including the passage of the USA PATRIOT Act), discusses in great depth the impact of technology on surveillance and citizen's rights, and proposes balancing between needed secrecy and oversight. We believe this is one of the most comprehensive articles addressing civil liberties issues in the context of national security research. We summarize some of the key points made in the article in the context of our proposed ISI research. Readers are strongly encouraged to refer to (Strickland et al., 2005) for more details.

Framed in the context of domestic security surveillance, the paper considers surveillance as an important intelligence tool that has the potential to contribute significantly to national security but also to infringe civil liberties. As faculty of the University of Maryland Information Science department, the authors believe that information science and technology has drastically expanded the mechanisms by which data can be collected, and knowledge extracted and disseminated through some automated means.

An immediate result of the tragic events of September 11, 2001, was the extraordinarily rapid passage of the USA PATRIOT Act in late 2001. The legislation was passed by the Senate on October 11, 2001, by the House on October 24, 2001, and signed by the President on October 26, 2001. The continuing legacy of the then-existing consensus and the lack of detailed debate and considerations created a bitter ongoing national argument as to the proper balance between national security and civil liberties. The PATRIOT Act contains ten titles in 131 pages. It amends numerous laws, including, for example, expansion of electronic surveillance of communications in law enforcement cases; authorizing sharing of law enforcement data with intelligence; expansion of the acquisition of electronic communications as well as commercial records for intelligence use; and creation of new terrorism-related crimes.

However, as new data mining and/or knowledge discovery techniques become mature and potentially useful for national security applications, there are great concerns of violating civil liberties. Both the DARPA's TIA Program and the Transportation Security Administration's (TSA) Computer Assisted Passenger Prescreening Systems (CAPPS II) were cited as failed systems that faced significant media scrutiny and public opposition. Both systems were based on extensive data mining of commercial and government databases collected for one purpose and to be shared and used for another purpose; and both systems were sidetracked by a widely perceived threat to personal privacy. Based on much of the debate generated by these programs, the authors suggest that data mining using public or private sector databases for national security purposes must proceed in two stages – first, the search for general information must ensure anonymity; second, the acquisition of specific identity, if required, must be by court order under appropriate standards (e.g., in terms of "special needs" or "probable causes").

In their concluding remarks, the authors cautioned that secrecy in any organization could pose a real risk of abuse and must be constrained through effective checks and balances. Moreover, information science and technology professionals are ideally situated to provide the tools and techniques by which the necessary intelligence is collected, analyzed, and disseminated; while civil liberties are protected through established laws and policies.

In addition to the review article by Strickland et al., readers are also referred to an excellent book entitled: *No Place to Hide*, written by Washington Post reporter Robert O'Harrow (O'Harrow, 2005). He reveals how the government is creating a national intelligence infrastructure with the help of private information, security, and technology companies. The book examines in detail the potential impact of this new national security system on our traditional notions of civil liberties, autonomy, and privacy.

2.5   Future Directions

National security research poses unique challenges and opportunities. Much of the established data mining and knowledge discovery literature, findings, and techniques need to be re-examined in light of the unique data and problem characteristics in the law enforcement and intelligence community. New text mining, spatial and temporal pattern mining, and criminal network analysis of relevance to national security are among some of the most pressing research areas. However, researchers cannot conduct research in a vacuum. Partnerships with local, state, and federal agencies need to be formed to obtain relevant test data and necessary domain expertise for ISI research. Only after rigorous testing with scrubbed or anonymous data can selected techniques be field examined and verified by the domain experts (i.e., law enforcement personnel, intelligence analysts, and policy makers). These techniques should be used in actual investigations only after experts have confirmed their potential value. At this stage, the researcher-designed algorithms or systems are often much improved and refined, and are often operated and controlled by the domain experts with their own heuristics, know-how, and judgment.

2.6   Questions for Discussion

1. What are the newest and most promising data mining techniques and approaches? How much of the data mining research can be conducted using existing tools and software and how much should be built from scratch?

2. How can new, promising, and unique data mining techniques for national security be identified? What are some ways to develop an integrated, multi-disciplinary research team for algorithms development, system development, user interface design, user assessment, and organizational impact study?

3. How can agency partners who are willing to collaborate, i.e., providing data and domain expertise, be identified? How should a win-win scenario for the research partnership be created?

4. What are some ways and places to find help on privacy and civil liberties issues? How can rigorous data mining research be conducted in consideration of civil liberties?

5. What are some ways to work with industry partners on national security research?

Chapter 3

ISI RESEARCH: LITERATURE REVIEW

Chapter Overview

In this chapter, we review the technical foundations of ISI and the six classes of data mining technologies specified in our ISI research framework: information sharing and collaboration, crime association mining, crime classification and clustering, intelligence text mining, spatial and temporal crime pattern mining, and criminal network analysis. We also summarize relevant research that addresses knowledge discovery in public safety and national security.

3.1 Information Sharing and Collaboration

Information sharing across jurisdictional boundaries of intelligence and security agencies has been identified as one of the key foundations for securing national security (Office of Homeland Security, 2002). However, sharing and integrating information from distributed, heterogeneous, and autonomous data sources is a non-trivial task (Hasselbring, 2000; Rahm and Bernstein, 2001). In addition to legal and cultural issues regarding information sharing, it is often difficult to integrate and combine data that are organized in different schemas and stored in different database systems running on different hardware platforms and operating systems (Hasselbring, 2000). Other data integration problems include: (1) name differences: same entity with different names; (2) mismatched domains: problems with units of measure or reference point; (3) missing data: incomplete data sources or different data available from different sources; and (4) object identification: no global ID values and no inter-database ID tables (Chen and Rotem, 1998).

Three approaches to data integration have been proposed: *federation*, *warehousing*, and *mediation* (Garcia-Molina et al., 2002). Database federation maintains data in their original, independent sources but provides a uniform data access mechanism (Buccella et al., 2003; Haas, 2002). Data warehousing is an integrated system in which copies of data from different data sources are migrated and stored to provide uniform access. Data mediation relies on "wrappers" to translate and pass queries from multiple data sources. The wrappers are "transparent" to an application so that the multiple databases appear to be a single database. These techniques are not mutually exclusive. Many hybrid approaches have been proposed (Jhingran et al., 2002).

All these techniques are dependent, to a great extent, on the matching between different databases. The task of database matching can be broadly divided into *schema-level* and *instance-level matching* (Lim et al., 1996; Rahm and Bernstein, 2001). Schema-level matching is performed by aligning semantically corresponding columns between two sources. Various schema elements such as attribute name, description, data type, and constraints may be used to generate a mapping between the two schemas (Rahm and Bernstein, 2001). For example, prior studies have used linguistic matchers to find similar attribute names based on synonyms, common substrings, pronunciation, and Soundex codes (Newcombe et al., 1959) to match attributes from different databases (Bell and Sethi, 2001). Instance-level or entity-level matching connects records describing a particular object in one database to records describing the same object in another database. Entity-level matching is frequently performed after schema-level matching is completed. Existing entity matching approaches include (1) key equivalence, (2) user specified equivalence, (3) probabilistic key equivalence, (4) probabilistic attribute equivalence, or (5) heuristic rules (Lim et al., 1996).

Some of these information integration approaches have been used in law enforcement and intelligence agencies for investigation support. The COPLINK Connect system (Chen et al., 2003b) employed the database federation approach to achieve schema-level data integration. It provided a common COPLINK schema and a one-stop-shopping user interface to facilitate the access of different data sources from multiple police departments. Evaluation results showed that COPLINK Connect had improved performance over the Record Management System (RMS) of police data in system effectiveness, ease of use, and interface design (Chen et al., 2003b). Similarly, the Phoenix Police Department Reports (PPDR) is a web-based, federated intelligence system in which databases shared common schema (Dolotov and Strickler, 2003). The Bioterrorism Surveillance Systems developed at the University of South Florida, on the other hand, used data warehouses to integrate historical and real-time surveillance data and incrementally incorporated data from diverse disease sources (Berndt et al., 2004; Berndt et al., 2003).

Integrating data at the entity level has also been difficult. In addition to existing key equivalence matching approaches and heuristic consolidation approaches (Goldberg and Senator, 1998), the use of the National Incident-Based Reporting System (NIBRS) (Federal Bureau of Investigation, 1992), a crime incident classification standard, has been proposed to enhance data sharing among law enforcement agencies (Faggiani and McLaughlin, 1999; Schroeder et al., 2003). In the Violent Crime Linkage Analysis System (ViCLAS) (Collins et al., 1998), data collection and encoding standards were used to capture more than 100 behavioral characteristics of offenders in serial violent crimes to address the problem of entity-level matching.

Information sharing has also been undertaken in intelligence and security agencies through cross-jurisdictional collaborative systems. COPLINK Agent was run on top of the COPLINK Connect system (Chen et al., 2003b) and linked crime investigators who were working on related crime cases at different units to enhance collaboration (Zeng et al., 2003). It employed collaborative filtering approaches (Goldberg et al., 1992), which have been widely studied in commercial recommender systems, to identify law enforcement users who had similar search histories. Similar search histories might indicate that these users had similar information needs and thus were working on related crime cases. When one user searched for information about a crime or a suspect, the system would alert other users who worked on related cases so that these users could collaborate and share their information through other communication channels. The FALCON system offered similar monitoring and alerting functionality (Brown, 1998b). Its collaboration capability, however, was relatively limited. Research has also been performed to mathematically model collaboration processes across law enforcement and intelligence jurisdictions to improve work productivity (Raghu et al., 2003; Zhao et al., 2003). Although information sharing and collaboration are not knowledge discovery *per se*, they prepare data for important subsequent analyses.

3.2   Crime Association Mining

Finding associations among data items is an important topic in knowledge discovery research. One of the most widely studied approaches is association rule mining, a process of discovering frequently occurring item sets in a database. Association rule mining is often used in market basket analysis where the objective is to find which products are bought with what other products (Agrawal et al., 1993; Mannila et al., 1994; Silverstein et al., 1998). An association is expressed as a rule X $\Rightarrow$ Y, indicating that item set X and item set Y occur together in the same transaction (Agrawal et al., 1993). Each rule is evaluated using two probability measures, *support* and *confidence*, where *support* is defined as $prob(X \cap Y)$ and *confidence* as $prob(X \cap Y)/prob(X)$. For example, "diapers $\Rightarrow$ milk with 60% *support* and 90% *confidence*" means that 60% of customers buy both diapers and milk in the same transaction and that 90% of the customers who buy diapers tend to also buy milk.

In the intelligence and security domain, spatial association rule mining (Koperski and Han, 1995) has been proposed to extract cause-effect relations among geographically referenced crime data to identify environmental factors that attract crimes (Estivill-Castro and Lee, 2001). Moreover, the research on association mining is not limited to association rule mining but covers the extraction of a wide variety of relationships among crime data items. Crime association mining techniques can include *incident association mining* and *entity association mining* (Lin and Brown, 2003).

The purpose of incident association mining is to find crimes that might be committed by the same offender so that unsolved crimes can be linked to solved crimes to identify the suspect. This technique is often used to solve serial crimes such as serial sexual offenses and serial homicide. However, finding associated crime incidents can be fairly time-consuming if it is performed manually. It is estimated that pairwise, manual comparisons on just a few hundred crime incidents would take more than 1 million human hours (Brown and Hagen, 2002). When the number of crime incidents is large, manual identification of associations between crimes is prohibitive in time. Two approaches, *similarity-based* and *outlier-based*, have been developed for incident association mining.

Similarity-based methods detect associations between crime incidents by comparing crimes' features such as spatial locations of the incidents and offenders' modus operandi (MO), which often are regarded as an offender's "behavioral signature" (O'Hara and O'Hara, 1980). Expert systems relying on decision rules acquired from domain experts used to be a common approach to associating crime incidents (Badiru et al., 1988; Bowen, 1994; Brahan et al., 1998). However, as the collection of human-decision rules requires a large amount of knowledge engineering effort and the rules collected are often hard to update, the expert system approach has been replaced by more automated approaches. Brown and Hagen (Brown and Hagen, 2002) developed a total similarity measure between two crime records as a weighted sum of similarities of various crime features. For features such as an offender's eye color that takes on categorical values, they developed a similarity table that specified the similarity level for each pair of categorical values based on heuristics. Evaluation showed that this approach enhanced both accuracy and efficiency for associating crime records. Similarly, Wang et al. (Wang et al., 2003) proposed to measure similarity between a new crime incident and existing criminal information stored in police databases by representing the new incident as a query and existing criminal information as vector spaces. The vector space model is widely employed in information retrieval applications and various similarity measures could be used (Rasmussen, 1992).

Unlike similarity-based methods which identify associations based on a number of crime features, the outlier-based method focuses only on the distinctive features of a crime (Lin and Brown, 2003). For example, in a series of robberies a Japanese sword was used as the weapon. Since a Japanese sword is a very uncommon weapon as opposed to other weapons such as shotguns, it is very likely that this series of robberies was committed by the same offender. Based on this outlier concept, crime investigators need to first cluster crime incidents into cells and then use an outlier score function to measure the distinctiveness of the incidents in a specific cell. If the outlier score of a cell is larger than a threshold value, the incidents contained in the cell are assumed to be associated and committed by the same offender. Evaluation showed that the outlier-based method was more effective than the similarity-based method proposed in (Brown and Hagen, 2002).

The task of finding and charting associations between crime entities such as persons, weapons, and organizations often is referred to as entity association mining (Lin and Brown, 2003) or link analysis (Sparrow, 1991) in law enforcement. The purpose is to find out how crime entities that appear to be unrelated at the surface are actually linked to each other. Law enforcement officers and crime investigators throughout the world have long used link analysis to search for and analyze relationships between criminals. For example, the Federal Bureau of Investigation (FBI) used link analysis in the investigation of the Oklahoma City Bombing case and the Unabomber case to look for criminal associations and investigative leads (Schroeder et al., 2003).

Three types of link analysis approaches have been suggested: *heuristic-based, statistical-based,* and *template-based.* Heuristic-based approaches rely on decision rules used by domain experts to determine whether two entities in question are related. For example, Goldberg and Senator (Goldberg and Senator, 1998) suggested that links or associations between individuals in financial transactions be created based on a set of heuristics, such as whether the individuals have shared addresses, shared bank accounts, or related transactions. This technique has been employed by the FinCEN system of the U.S. Department of the Treasury to detect money laundering transactions and activities (Goldberg and Senator, 1998; Goldberg and Wong, 1998). The COPLINK Detect system (Hauck et al., 2002) employed a statistical-based approach called Concept Space (Chen and Lynch, 1992). This approach measures the weighted co-occurrence associations between records of entities (persons, organizations, vehicles, and locations) stored in crime databases. An association exists between a pair of entities if they appear together in the same criminal incident. The more frequently they occur together, the stronger the association is. Zhang et al. (Zhang et al., 2003) proposed to use a fuzzy resemblance function to calculate the correlation between two individuals' past financial transactions to detect associations between the individuals who might have been involved in a specific money laundering crime. If the correlation between two individuals is higher than a threshold value these two individuals are regarded as being related. The template-based approach has been primarily used to identify associations between entities extracted from textual documents such as police report narratives. Lee (Lee, 1998) developed a template-based technique using relation-specifying words and phrases. For example, the phrase "member of" indicates an entity-entity association between an individual and an organization. Coady (Coady, 1985) proposed to use the PROLOG language to automatically derive rules of entity associations from text data and use the rules to detect associations in similar documents. Template-based approaches heavily rely on a fixed set of predefined patterns and rules, and thus may have a limited scope of application.

3.3   Crime Classification and Clustering

Classification is the process of mapping data items into one of several predefined categories based on attribute values of the items (Hand, 1981; Weiss and Kulikowski, 1991). Examples of classification applications include fraud detection (Chan and Stolfo, 1998), computer and network intrusion detection (Lee and Stolfo, 1998), bank failure prediction (Sarkar and Sriram, 2001), and image categorization (Fayyad et al., 1996). Classification is a type of supervised learning that consists of a training stage and a testing stage. Accordingly the dataset is divided into a training set and a testing set. The classifier is designed to "learn" from the training set classification models governing the membership of data items. Accuracy of the classifier is assessed using the testing set.

Discriminant analysis (Eisenbeis and Avery, 1972), Bayesian models (Duda and Hart, 1973; Heckerman, 1995), decision trees (Quinlan, 1986, 1993), artificial neural networks (Rumelhart et al., 1986), and support vector machines (SVM) (Vapnik, 1995) are widely used classification techniques. In discriminant analysis, the class membership of a data item is modeled as a function of the item's attribute values. Through regression analysis, a class membership discriminant function can be obtained and used to classify new data items.

Bayesian classifiers assume all data attributes are conditionally independent given the class membership outcome. The task is to learn the conditional probabilities among the attributes given the class membership outcome. The learned model is then used to predict the class membership of new data items based on their attribute values.

Decision tree classifiers organize decision rules learned from training data in the form of a tree. Algorithms such as ID3 (Quinlan, 1986, 1993) and C4.5 (Quinlan, 1993) are popular decision tree classifiers.

An artificial neural network consists of interconnected nodes to imitate the functioning of neurons and synapses of human brains. It usually contains an input layer, with nodes taking on the attribute values of the data items, and an output layer, with nodes representing the class membership labels. Neural networks learn and encode knowledge through the connection weights.

SVM is a novel learning classifier based on the Structural Risk Minimization principle from the computational learning theory. SVM is capable of handling millions of inputs and does not require feature selection (Cristianini and Shawe-Taylor, 2000). Each of these classification techniques has its advantages and disadvantages in terms of accuracy, efficiency, and interpretability. Researchers have also proposed hybrid approaches to combine these techniques (Kumar and Olmeda, 1999).

Several of these techniques have been applied in the intelligence and security domain to detect financial fraud and computer network intrusion. For example, to identify fraudulent financial transactions Aleskerov et al. (Aleskerov et al., 1997) employed neural networks to detect anomalies in customers' credit card transactions based on their transaction history. Hassibi (Hassibi, 2000) employed a feed-forward back-propagation neural network to compute the probability that a given transaction was fraudulent.

Two types of intrusion detection, *misuse detection* and *anomaly detection*, have been studied in computer network security applications (Lee and Stolfo, 1998). Misuse detection identifies attacks by matching them to previously known attack patterns or signatures. Anomaly detection, on the other hand, identifies abnormal user behaviors based on historical data. Lee and Stolfo (Lee and Stolfo, 1998) employed decision rule induction approaches to classify *sendmail* system call traces into normal or abnormal traces. Ryan et al. (Ryan et al., 1998) developed a neural network-based intrusion detection system to detect unusual user activity based on the patterns of users' past system command usage. Stolfo et al. (Stolfo et al., 2003) applied Bayesian classifiers to distinguish between normal email and spamming email.

Unlike classification, clustering is a type of unsupervised learning. It groups similar data items into clusters without knowing their class membership. The basic principle is to maximize intra-cluster similarity while minimizing inter-cluster similarity (Jain et al., 1999). Clustering has been used in a variety of applications, including image segmentation (Jain and Flynn, 1996), gene clustering (Eisen et al., 1998), and document categorization (Chen et al., 1998; Chen et al., 1996). Various clustering methods have been developed, including *hierarchical approaches* such as complete-link algorithms (Defays, 1977), *partitional approaches* such as *k*-means (Anderberg, 1973; Kohonen, 1995), and *Self-Organizing Maps* (SOM) (Kohonen, 1995). These clustering methods group data items based on different criteria and may not generate the same clustering results. Hierarchical clustering groups data items into a series of nested clusters and generates a tree-like dendrogram. Partitional clustering algorithms generate only one partition level rather than nested clusters. Partitional clustering is more efficient and scalable for large datasets than hierarchical clustering, but has the problem of determining the appropriate number of clusters (Jain et al., 1999). Different from the hierarchical and partitional clustering that relies on the similarity or proximity measures between data items, SOM is a neural network-based approach that directly projects multivariate data items onto two-dimensional maps. SOM can be used for clustering and visualizing data items and groups (Chen et al., 1996).

The use of clustering methods in the law enforcement and security domains can be categorized into two types: *crime incident clustering* and *criminal clustering*. The purpose of crime incident clustering is to find a set of similar crime incidents based on an offender's behavioral traits or to find a geographical area with a high concentration of certain types of crimes. For example, Adderley and Musgrove (Adderley and Musgrove, 2001) employed the SOM approach to cluster sexual attack crimes based on a number of offender MO attributes (e.g., the precaution methods taken and the verbal themes during the crime) to identify serial sexual offenders. The clusters found were used to form offender profiles containing MO and other information such as offender motives and racial preferences when choosing victims. Similarly, Kangas et al. (Kangas et al., 2003) employed the SOM method to group crime incidents to identify serial murderers and sexual offenders. Brown (Brown, 1998a) proposed *k*-means and the nearest neighbor approach to clustering spatial data of crimes to find "hotspot" areas in a city. The spatial clustering methods are often used in "hotspot analysis," which will be reviewed in detail in Section 3.5.

Criminal clustering is often used to identify groups of criminals who are closely related. Instead of using similarity measures, this type of clustering relies on relational strength that measures the intensiveness and frequency of relationships between offenders. Stolfo et al. (Stolfo et al., 2003) proposed to group email users that frequently communicate with each other into clusters so that unusual email behavior that violated the group communication patterns could be effectively detected. Offender clustering is more often used in criminal network analysis, which will be reviewed in detail in Section 3.6.

3.4   Intelligence Text Mining

A large amount of intelligence- and security-related data is represented in text forms such as police narrative reports, court transcripts, news clips, and web articles. Valuable information in such texts is often difficult to retrieve, access, and use for the purposes of crime investigation and counter-terrorism. It is desirable to automatically mine the text data to discover valuable knowledge about criminal or terrorism activities.

Text mining has attracted increasing attention in recent years as natural language processing capabilities advance (Chen, 2001). An important task of text mining is information extraction, a process of identifying and extracting from free text select types of information such as entities, relationships, and events (Grishman, 2003). The most widely studied information extraction subfield is named-entity extraction. It helps automatically identify from text documents the names of entities of interest, such as persons (e.g., "John Doe"), locations (e.g., "Washington, D.C."), and organizations (e.g.,

"National Science Foundation"). It has also been extended to identify other text patterns, such as dates, times, number expressions, dollar amounts, email addresses, and web addresses (URLs). The Message Understanding Conference (MUC) series has been the major forum for researchers in this area, where researchers meet and compare the performance of their entity extraction approaches (Chinchor, 1998).

Four major named-entity extraction approaches have been proposed: lexical-lookup, rule-based, statistical model, and machine learning.

- *Lexical lookup*. Most research systems maintain hand-crafted lexicons that contain lists of popular names for entities of interest, such as all registered organization names in the U.S., all person last names obtained from the government census data, etc. These systems work by looking up phrases in texts that match the items specified in their lexicons (Borthwick et al., 1998).

- *Rule-based*. Rule-based systems rely on hand-crafted rules to identify named entities. The rules may be structural, contextual, or lexical (Krupka and Hausman, 1998). An example rule would look like the following:
  capitalized last name + , + capitalized first name ⇒ *person name*
  Although such human-created rules are usually of high quality, this approach may not be easy to apply to other entity types.

- *Statistical model*. Such systems often use statistical models to identify occurrences of certain cues or particular patterns for entities in texts. A training dataset is needed for a system to obtain the statistics. The statistical language model reported in (Witten et al., 1999) is an example for such systems.

- *Machine learning*. This type of system relies on machine learning algorithms rather than human-created rules to extract knowledge or identify patterns from text data. Examples of machine learning algorithms used in entity extraction include neural networks, decision trees (Baluja et al., 1999), Hidden Markov Model (Miller et al., 1998), and entropy maximization (Borthwick et al., 1998).

Instead of relying on a single approach, most existing information extraction systems utilize a combination of two or more of these approaches. Many systems were evaluated at the MUC-7 Conference. The best systems were able to achieve over 90% in both precision and recall rates in extracting persons, locations, organizations, dates, times, currencies, and percentages.

Recent years have seen research on named-entity extraction for intelligence and security applications (Patman and Thompson, 2003; Wang et al., 2004b). For example, Chau et al. (Chau et al., 2002) developed a neural network-based entity extraction system to identify person names, addresses, narcotic drugs, and personal property names from police report narratives. Rather than relying entirely on manual rule generation, this system combines lexical lookup, machine learning, and some hand-crafted rules. The system achieved over 70% precision and recall rates for person name and narcotic drug names. However, it was difficult to achieve satisfactory performance for addresses and personal properties because of their wide coverage. Sun et al. (Sun et al., 2003) converted the entity extraction problem into a classification problem to identify relevant entities from the MUC text collection in the terrorism domain. They first identified all noun phrases in a document and then used the support vector machine to classify these entity candidates based on both content and context features. The results showed that for the specific terrorism text collection the approach's performance in precision and F measure was comparable with AutoSlog (Riloff, 1996), one of the best entity extraction systems.

Several news and event extraction systems have been reported recently, including Columbia's Newsblaster (McKeown et al., 2003) and Carnegie Mellon University's system (Yang et al., 1999), which automatically extract, categorize, and summarize events from international online news sources. Some of these systems can also work for multilingual documents and have great potential for automatic detection and tracking of terrorism events for intelligence purposes.

3.5   Crime Spatial and Temporal Mining

Most crimes, including terrorism, have significant spatial and temporal characteristics (Brantingham and Brantingham, 1981). Analysis of spatial and temporal patterns of crimes has been one of the most important crime investigation techniques. It aims to gather intelligence about environmental factors that prevent or encourage crimes (Brantingham and Brantingham, 1981), identify geographic areas of high crime concentration (Levine, 2000), and detect crime trends (Schumacher and Leitner, 1999). With the patterns found, effective and proactive control strategies, such as allocating the appropriate amount of police resources in certain areas at certain times, may be selected to prevent crimes.

Spatial pattern analysis and geographical profiling of crimes play important roles in solving crimes (Rosmo, 1995). Three approaches for crime spatial pattern mining have been reported: *visual approach*, *clustering approaches*, and *statistical approaches* (Murray et al., 2001). The visual approach is also called crime mapping. It presents a city or region map annotated with various crime-related information. For example, a map can be color-coded to present the densities of a specific type of crime in different geographical areas. Such an approach can help users visually detect the relationship between spatial features and crime occurrences.

The clustering approach has been used in hotspot analysis, a process of automatically identifying areas with high crime concentration. This type of analysis helps law enforcement effectively allocate police efforts to reduce crimes in hotspot areas. Partitional clustering algorithms such as the k-means methods are often used for finding crime hotspots (Murray and Estivill-Castro, 1998). For example, Schumacher and Leitner (Schumacher and Leitner, 1999) used the k-means algorithm to identify hotspots in the downtown areas of Baltimore. Comparing the hotspots of different years, they found spatial patterns of the displacement of crimes after redevelopment of the downtown area. Corresponding proactive strategies were then suggested based on the patterns found. Although they are efficient and scalable compared with hierarchical clustering algorithms, partitional clustering algorithms usually require the user to predefine the number of clusters to be found. This is not always feasible, however (Grubesic and Murray, 2001). Accordingly, researchers have tried to use statistical approaches to conduct hotspot analysis or to test the significance of hotspots (Craglia et al., 2000). The test statistics G_i (Getis and Ord, 1992; Ord and Getis, 1995) and Moran's I (Moran, 1950), which are used to test the significance of spatial autocorrelation, can be used to detect hotspots. If a variable is correlated with itself through space it is said to be spatially autocorrelated. For example, Ratchliffe and McCullagh (Ratchliffe and McCullagh, 1999) employed the G_i and G_i^* statistics to identify the hotspots of residential burglary and motor vehicle crimes in a city. Compared with a domain expert's perception of the hotspots, this approach was shown to be effective.

Statistical approaches have also been used in crime prediction applications. Based on the spatial choice theory (McFadden, 1973), Xue and Brown (Xue and Brown, 2003) modeled the probability of a criminal choosing a target location as a function of multiple spatial characteristics of the location such as family density per unit area and distance to highway. Using regression analysis they predicted the locations of future crimes in a city. Evaluation showed that their models significantly outperformed conventional hotspot models. Similarly, Brown et al. (Brown et al., 2004) built a logistic regression model to predict suicide bombing in counter-terrorism applications.

Commercially available graphical information systems (GIS) and crime mapping tools such as ArcView and MapInfo have been widely used in law enforcement and intelligence agencies for analyzing and visualizing spatial patterns of crimes. Geographical coordinate information as well as various spatial features, such as the distance between the location of a crime to major roads and police stations, is often used in GIS (Harris, 1990; Weisburd and McEwen, 1997).

Research on temporal patterns of crimes is relatively scarce in comparison to crime mapping. Two major approaches have been reported, namely *visualization* and the *statistical approach*. Visualization approaches present individual or aggregated temporal features of crimes using periodic view or timeline view. Common methods for viewing periodic data include sequence charts, point charts, bar charts, line charts, and spiral graphs displayed in 2D or 3D (Tufte, 1983). In a timeline view, a sequence of events is presented based on its temporal order. For example, LifeLines provides the visualization of a patient's medical history using a timeline view. The Spatial Temporal Visualizer (STV) (Buetow et al., 2003) seamlessly incorporated periodic view, timeline view, and GIS view in the system to provide support to crime investigations. Visualization approaches rely on human users to interpret data presentations and to find temporal patterns of events. Statistical approaches, on the other hand, build statistical models from observations to capture the temporal patterns of events. For instance, Brown and Oxford (Brown and Oxford, 2001) developed several statistical models, including log-normal regression model, Poisson regression model, and cumulative logistic regression model, to predict the number of breaking and entering crimes. The log-normal regression model was found to fit the data best (Brown and Oxford, 2001).

3.6   Criminal Network Analysis

Criminals seldom operate alone but instead interact with one another to carry out various illegal activities. Relationships between individual offenders form the basis for organized crime and are essential for the effective operation of a criminal enterprise. Criminal enterprises can be viewed as a network consisting of nodes (individual offenders) and links (relationships). In criminal networks, groups or teams may exist within which members have close relationships. One group also may interact with other groups to obtain or transfer illicit goods. Moreover, individuals play different roles in their groups. For example, some key members may act as leaders to control the activities of a group. Some others may serve as gatekeepers to ensure the smooth flow of information or illicit goods.

Structural network patterns in terms of subgroups, between-group interactions, and individual roles thus are important to understanding the organization, structure, and operation of criminal enterprises. Such knowledge can help law enforcement and intelligence agencies disrupt criminal networks and develop effective control strategies to combat organized crimes. For example, removal of central members in a network may effectively upset the operational network and put a criminal enterprise out of action (Baker and Faulkner, 1993; McAndrew, 1999; Sparrow, 1991). Subgroups and interaction patterns between groups are helpful for finding a network's overall structure, which often reveals points of vulnerability (Evan, 1972; Ronfeldt and Arquilla, 2001). For a centralized structure such as a star or a wheel, the point of vulnerability lies in its central members. A decentralized network such as a chain or clique, however, does not have a single point of vulnerability and thus may be more difficult to disrupt.

Social Network Analysis (SNA) provides a set of measures and approaches for structural network analysis (Wasserman and Faust, 1994). These techniques were originally designed to discover social structures in social networks (Wasserman and Faust, 1994) and are especially appropriate for studying criminal networks (McAndrew, 1999; Sparrow, 1991). Studies involving evidence mapping in fraud and conspiracy cases have employed SNA measures to identify central members in criminal networks (Baker and Faulkner, 1993; Saether and Canter, 2001). In general, SNA is capable of detecting subgroups, identifying central individuals, discovering between-group interaction patterns, and uncovering a network's structure.

- *Subgroup detection.* With networks represented in a matrix format, the matrix permutation approach and cluster analysis have been employed to detect underlying groups that are not otherwise apparent in data (Wasserman and Faust, 1994). Burt (Burt, 1976) proposed to apply hierarchical clustering methods based on a structural equivalence measure (Lorrain and White, 1971) to partition a social network into positions in which members have similar structural roles. Xu and Chen (Xu and Chen, 2003) employed hierarchical clustering to detect criminal groups in narcotics networks based on the relational strength between criminals.

- *Central member identification.* Centrality deals with the roles of network members. Several measures, such as degree, betweenness, and closeness, are related to centrality (Freeman, 1979). The *degree* of a particular node is its number of direct links; its *betweenness* is the number of geodesics (shortest paths between any two nodes) passing through it; and its *closeness* is the sum of all the geodesics between the particular node and every other node in the network. Although these three measures are all intended to illustrate the importance or centrality of a node, they interpret the roles of network members differently. An individual having a high degree measurement, for instance, may be inferred to have a leadership function, whereas an individual with a high level of betweenness may be seen as a gatekeeper in the network. Baker and Faulkner employed these three measures, especially degree, to find the key individuals in a price-fixing conspiracy network in the electrical equipment industry (Baker and Faulkner, 1993). Krebs found that, in the network consisting of the nineteen September 11th hijackers, Mohamed Atta had the highest degree score (Krebs, 2001).

- *Discovery of patterns of interaction.* Patterns of interaction between subgroups can be discovered using an SNA approach called blockmodel analysis (Arabie et al., 1978). Given a partitioned network, blockmodel analysis determines the presence or absence of an association between a pair of subgroups by comparing the density of the links between them at a predefined threshold value. In this way, blockmodeling introduces summarized individual interaction details into interactions between groups so that the overall structure of the network becomes more apparent.

SNA also includes visualization methods that present networks graphically. The Smallest Space Analysis (SSA) approach (Wasserman and Faust, 1994), a branch of Multi-Dimensional Scaling (MDS), is used extensively in SNA to produce two-dimensional representations of social networks. In a graphical portrayal of a network produced by SSA, the stronger the association between two nodes or two groups, the closer they appear on the graph; the weaker the association, the farther apart they are (McAndrew, 1999). Several network analysis tools, such as Analyst's Notebook (Klerks, 2001), Netmap (Goldberg and Senator, 1998), and Watson (Anderson et al., 1994), can automatically draw a graphical representation of a criminal network. However, they do not provide much structural analysis functionality and rely on investigators' manual examinations to extract structural patterns.

The above-reviewed six classes of KDD techniques constitute the key components of our proposed ISI research framework. Our focus on the KDD methodology, however, does not exclude other approaches. For example, studies using simulation and multi-agent models have shown promise in the "what-if" analysis of the robustness of terrorist and criminal networks (Carley et al., 2003; Carley et al., 2002).

3.7   Future Directions

There are many opportunities for researchers from different disciplines to contribute to the science of ISI. Computer science researchers in databases, artificial intelligence, data mining, algorithms, networking, and grid computing are poised to contribute significantly to core information infrastructure, integration, and analysis research of relevance to ISI. Information systems, information science, and management science researchers could help develop the quantitative, system, and information theory-based methodologies needed for the systematic study of national security. Cognitive science, behavioral research, management and policy, and legal disciplines are critical to the understanding of the individual, group, organizational, and societal impacts and the creation of effective national security policies. All the abovementioned academic disciplines need to work closely with the domain experts in law enforcement, public safety, emergency response, and the intelligence community.

3.8 Questions for Discussion

1. What are the core technical foundations for ISI research? What are the undergraduate and graduate courses in various disciplines that can help contribute to this understanding?

2. What are the major conferences, journals, and magazines that publish and promote ISI research? Are there professional ISI-related societies or work groups?

3. What are the major research centers, laboratories, non-profit agencies, and government programs that provide training, education, and research resources of relevance to ISI?

4. Are there government sponsored national security-related training and fellowship programs? What about some of the intern, co-op, and employment opportunities for an IT career in national security?

Chapter 4
NATIONAL SECURITY CRITICAL MISSION AREAS AND CASE STUDIES

Chapter Overview

This chapter provides an overview for the next six chapters. Based on research conducted at the University of Arizona's Artificial Intelligence Lab and its affiliated NSF COPLINK Center for Law Enforcement and Intelligence Research, we review seventeen case studies that are relevant to the six homeland security critical mission areas described earlier. More details about each case study follow in each of the next six chapters.

4.1 Introduction

In response to the challenges of national security, the Artificial Intelligence Lab and its affiliated NSF COPLINK Center for Law Enforcement and Intelligence Research at the University of Arizona have developed many research projects over the past decade to address the six critical mission areas identified in the "National Strategy for Homeland Security" report (Office of Homeland Security, 2002): *intelligence and warning, border and transportation security, domestic counter-terrorism, protecting critical infrastructure and key assets, defending against catastrophic terrorism,* and *emergency preparedness and responses.* The main goal of the Arizona lab/center is to develop information and knowledge management technologies appropriate for capturing, accessing, analyzing, visualizing, and sharing law enforcement- and intelligence-related information (Chen et al., 2003c).

We demonstrate through seventeen case studies how critical mission issues could be addressed using the knowledge discovery approach. For each case study we discuss its relevance to national security missions, data characteristics, technologies used, and select evaluation results. Quantitative studies focused primarily on the performance of the techniques in terms of effectiveness, accuracy, efficiency, usefulness, etc. In qualitative studies, we summarize and report comments and feedback from our domain experts. We also suggest further readings for each case study.

4.2 Intelligence and Warning

Detecting potential terrorist attacks or crimes is possible and feasible with the help of information technology. By analyzing the communication and activity patterns among terrorists and their contacts (i.e., terrorist networks), detecting deceptive identities, or employing other surveillance and monitoring techniques, intelligence and warning systems may issue timely, critical alerts to prevent attacks or crimes from occurring.

We present four case studies of relevance to intelligence and warning in Chapter 5. In Case Study 1, we report a taxonomy of identity deceptions based on police criminal records and propose an entity-matching technique to detect deception. In Case Study 2, we report on the Dark Web Portal project, which collects open source terrorism web site information based on select spidering and portal techniques. Case Study 3 summarizes web spidering and link analysis techniques adopted to analyze the presence of the Jihad on the web. Based on high-quality open source (news) generated terrorist information, Case Study 4 summarizes topological analysis research performed for the Al-Qaeda terrorist network.

Table 4-1. Case studies in intelligence and warning.

Case Study	Project	Data Characteristics	Technologies Used	Critical Mission Area Addressed
1	Detecting deceptive identities	• Authoritative source • Structured criminal identity records	• Association mining	Intelligence and warning
2	Dark Web Portal	• Open source • Web hyperlink data	• Web spidering and archiving • Portal access	Intelligence and warning
3	Jihad on the Web	• Open source • Multilingual, web data	• Web spidering • Multilingual indexing • Link and content analysis	Intelligence and warning
4	Analyzing al Qaeda network	• Open source • News articles	• Statistics-based • Network topological analysis	Intelligence and warning

For more details about case studies described above, readers are referred to:

- G. Wang, H. Chen, and H. Atabakhsh, "Automatically Detecting Deceptive Criminal Identities," *Communications of the ACM*, Volume 47, Number 3, Pages 71-76, 2004.

- G. Wang, H. Chen, and H. Atabakhsh, "Criminal Identity Deception and Deception Detection in Law Enforcement," *Group Decision and Negotiation*, Volume 13, Number 2, Pages 111-127, 2004.

- E. Reid, J. Qin, W. Chung, J. Xu, Y. Zhou, R. Schumaker, M. Sageman, and H. Chen, "Terrorism Knowledge Discovery Project: A Knowledge Discovery Approach to Addressing the Threats of Terrorism," *Intelligence and Security Informatics*, Proceedings of the Second Symposium on Intelligence and Security Informatics, ISI 2004, Tucson, Arizona, June 2004, Lecture Notes in Computer Science (LNCS 3073), Springer-Verlag.

- H. Chen, J. Qin, E. Reid, W. Chung, Y. Zhou, W. Xi, G. Lai, A. Bonillas, F. Wang, and M. Sageman, "The Dark Web Portal: Collecting and Analyzing the Presence of Domestic and International Terrorist Groups in the Web," *Proceedings of the 7th IEEE International Conference on Intelligent Transportation Systems (ITSC 2004)*, Washington, DC, October 3-6, 2004.

4.3   Border and Transportation Security

We believe that we can greatly improve the capabilities of counter-terrorism and crime-fighting by creating a "smart border," where information from multiple sources is integrated and analyzed to help locate wanted terrorists or criminals. Technologies such as information sharing and integration, collaboration and communication, and biometrics and speech recognition will be greatly needed in such smart borders.

As shown in Table 4-2, Chapter 6 will review two case studies of relevance to border and transportation security. Case Study 5 reports on the BorderSafe project's information sharing and integration effort based on multiple local law enforcement criminal incident records. Case Study 6 reports topological network analysis performed on several cross-jurisdictional narcotic networks in the Southwest.

Table 4-2. Case studies in border and transportation security.

Case Study	Project	Data Characteristics	Technologies Used	Critical Mission Area Addressed
5	BorderSafe information sharing	• Authoritative source • Structured criminal identity records	• Information sharing and integration • Database federation	Border and transportation security
6	Cross-border network analysis	• Authoritative source • Structured criminal identify records	• Network topological analysis	Border and transportation security

For more details about case studies described above, readers are referred to:

- H. Chen, F. Y. Wang, and D. Zeng, "Intelligence and Security Informatics for Homeland Security: Information, Communication, and Transportation," *IEEE Transactions on Intelligent Transportation Systems,* Volume 5, Number 4, Pages 329-341, 2004.

- B. Marshall, S. Kaza, J. Xu, H. Atabakhsh, T. Peterson, C. Violette, and H. Chen, "Cross-jurisdictional Criminal Activity Networks to Support Border and Transportation Security," *Proceedings of the 7th IEEE International Conference on Intelligent Transportation Systems (ITSC 2004),* Washington, DC, October 3-6, 2004.

4.4   Domestic Counter-terrorism

As terrorists, both international and domestic, may be involved in local crimes, state and local law enforcement agencies are also contributing to the homeland security missions by investigating and prosecuting crimes. Information technologies that help find cooperative relationships between criminals and their interactive patterns would also be helpful for analyzing domestic terrorism.

Table 4-3 summarizes four case studies of relevance to counter-terrorism research (reported in Chapter 7). Case Study 7 reports on the COPLINK Detect system that helps identify criminal associations based on law enforcement data. Case Study 8 reports on gang and narcotic criminal networks analysis based on selected social network analysis and clustering techniques. Case Study 9 reports how domestic extremist groups use the web to disseminate their ideology, recruit members, and support communications. Case Study 10 reports on a network topological study that analyzes various dark networks including: narcotic networks, terrorist networks, and terrorist web sites.

Table 4-3. Case studies in domestic counter-terrorism.

Case Study	Project	Data Characteristics	Technologies Used	Critical Mission Area Addressed
7	COPLINK Detect	• Authoritative source • Structured data	• Association mining	Domestic counter-terrorism
8	Criminal network analysis	• Authoritative source • Structured data	• Social network analysis • Cluster analysis • Visualization	Domestic counter-terrorism
9	Domestic extremists on the web	• Open source • Web-based text data	• Web spidering • Link and content analysis	Domestic counter-terrorism
10	Dark networks analysis	• Authoritative and open sources	• Network topological analysis	Domestic counter-terrorism

For more details about case studies described above, readers are referred to:

- R. V. Hauck, H. Atabakhsh, P. Ongvasith, H. Gupta, and H. Chen, "Using Coplink to Analyze Criminal-Justice Data," *IEEE Computer,* Volume 35, Number 3, Pages 30-37, 2002.

- H. Chen, J. Schroeder, R. V. Hauck, L. Ridgeway, H. Atabakhsh, H. Gupta, C. Boarman, K. Rasmussen, and A. W. Clements, "COPLINK

Connect: Information and Knowledge Management for Law Enforcement," *Decision Support Systems,* Special Issue on Digital Government, Volume 34, Number 3, Pages 271-286, February 2003.

- H. Chen, D. Zeng, H. Atabakhsh, W. Wyzga, J. Schroeder, "COPLINK: Managing Law Enforcement Data and Knowledge," *Communications of the ACM,* Volume 46, Number 1, Pages 28-34, January 2003.

- H. Chen, W. Chung, J. Xu, G. Wang, M. Chau, Y. Qin, and M. Chau, "Crime Data Mining: A General Framework and Some Examples," *IEEE Computer,* Volume 37, Number 4, Pages 50-56, 2004.

- J. Xu and H. Chen, "Fighting Organized Crimes: Using Shortest-Path Algorithms to Identify Associations in Criminal Networks," *Decision Support Systems,* Volume 38, Number 3, Pages 473-488, 2004.

- H. Chen, F. Y. Wang, and D. Zeng, "Intelligence and Security Informatics for Homeland Security: Information, Communication, and Transportation," *IEEE Transactions on Intelligent Transportation Systems,* Volume 5, Number 4, Pages 329-341, 2004.

- H. Chen, J. Qin, E. Reid, W. Chung, Y. Zhou, W. Xi, G. Lai, A. Bonillas, F. Wang, and M. Sageman "The Dark Web Portal: Collecting and Analyzing the Presence of Domestic and International Terrorist Groups in the Web," *Proceedings of the 7th IEEE International Conference on Intelligent Transportation Systems (ITSC 2004),* Washington, DC, October 3-6, 2004.

4.5 Protecting Critical Infrastructure and Key Assets

Cyber infrastructure such as the Internet may be vulnerable to intrusions and inside threats. Criminals and terrorists are increasingly using cyberspace to conduct illegal activities, share ideology, solicit funding, and recruit. In addition to physical devices such as sensors and detectors, advanced information technologies are needed to model the normal behaviors of the usage of these systems and then use the models to distinguish abnormal behaviors from normal behaviors. One aspect of protecting cyber infrastructure is to determine the source and identity of unwanted threats or intrusions.

We report on three case studies relevant to authorship identification based on multilingual messages (e.g., email and bulletin board messages) posted on the Internet. Case Study 11 reports authorship language models developed in English and Chinese. Case Study 12 reports how selected "writeprint" features are determined based on feature selection techniques.

Case Study 13 reports a novel Arabic language model for authorship identification.

Table 4-4. Case studies in protecting critical infrastructure.

Case Study	Project	Data Characteristics	Technologies Used	Critical Mission Area Addressed
11	Identity tracing in cyberspace	• Open source • Multilingual, text, web data	• Feature extraction • Classifications	Protecting critical infrastructure
12	Writeprint feature selection	• Open source • Multilingual, text, web data	• Feature extraction • Feature selection	Protecting critical infrastructure
13	Arabic authorship analysis	• Open source • Multilingual, text, web data	• Feature extraction • Classifications	Protecting critical infrastructure

For more details about case studies described above, readers are referred to:

- R. Zheng, Y. Qin, Z. Huang, and H. Chen, "Authorship Analysis in Cybercrime Investigation," Proceedings of the 1st NSF/NIJ Symposium on Intelligence and Security Informatics, ISI 2003, Tucson, Arizona, June 2003, Lecture Notes in Computer Science (LNCS 2665), Springer-Verlag.

- J. Li, R. Zheng, and H. Chen, "From Fingerprint to Writeprint," *Communications of the ACM*, forthcoming, 2005.

- R. Zheng, J. Li, H. Chen, Z. Huang, and Q. Yi, "A Framework of Authorship Identification for Online Messages: Writing Style Features and Classification Techniques," *Journal of the American Society for Information Science and Technology* (*JASIST*), forthcoming, 2005.

4.6   Defending Against Catastrophic Terrorism

Biological attacks may cause contamination, infectious disease outbreaks, and significant loss of life. Information systems that can efficiently and effectively collect, access, analyze, and report data about catastrophe-leading events can help prevent, detect, respond to, and manage these attacks. Case Study 14 reports on the BioPortal project that aims to develop an infectious disease and bioagent information sharing and analysis framework. Select West Nile Virus, botulism, and foot-and-mouth disease data from several state public heath departments have been incorporated. Case Study 15 reports research that compares several hotspot analysis methods for disease surveillance.

Table 4-5. Case studies in defending against catastrophic terrorism.

Case Study	Project	Data Characteristics	Technologies Used	Critical Mission Area Addressed
14	BioPortal for informa-tion sharing	• Authoritative source • Structured data	• Information integration and messaging • GIS analysis and visualization	Defending against catastrophic terrorism
15	Hotspot analysis	• Authoritative source • Structured data	• Statistics-based SatScan • Clustering; SVM	Defending against catastrophic terrorism

For more details about case studies described above, readers are referred to:

- D. Zeng, H. Chen, C. Tseng, C. Larson, M. Eidson, I. Gotham, C. Lynch, and M. Ascher, "Towards a National Infectious Disease Information Infrastructure: A Case Study in West Nile Virus and Botulism," Proceedings of the National Conference on Digital Government Research, DG.O 2004, Seattle, Washington, May 2004, Digital Government Research Center.

- D. Zeng, H. Chen, C. Tseng, C. Larson, M. Eidson, I. Gotham, C. Lynch, and M. Ascher, "West Nile Virus and Botulism Portal: A Case Study in Infectious Disease Informatics," *Intelligence and Security Informatics*, Proceedings of the Second Symposium on Intelligence and Security Informatics, ISI 2004, Tucson, Arizona, June 2004, Lecture Notes in Computer Science (LNCS 3073), Springer-Verlag.

- D. Zeng, W. Chang, and H. Chen, "A Comparative Analysis of Spatio-Temporal Hotspot Analysis Techniques in Security Informatics," *Proceedings of the 7th IEEE International Conference on Intelligent Transportation Systems (ITSC 2004)*, Washington, DC, October 3-6, 2004.

- H. Chen, F. Y. Wang, and D. Zeng, "Intelligence and Security Informatics for Homeland Security: Information, Communication, and Transportation," *IEEE Transactions on Intelligent Transportation Systems,* Volume 5, Number 4, Pages 329-341, 2004.

4.7 Emergency Preparedness and Response

In addition to systems that are designed to defend against catastrophes, information technologies that help optimize response plans, identify experts, train response professionals, and manage consequences are beneficial in the long run. Moreover, information systems that provide social and psychological support to the victims of terrorist attacks can also help society recover from disasters.

We summarize two case studies in Table 4-6. Case Study 16 reports on the terrorism expert finder project that identifies key terrorism researchers and their co-authorship relationships based on bibliometric analysis. Case Study 17 reports a terrorism information interface based on the ALICE chatterbot technology that facilitates human-like dialog.

Table 4-6. Case studies in emergency preparedness and responses.

Case Study	Project	Data Characteristics	Technologies Used	Critical Mission Area Addressed
16	Terrorism expert finder	• Open source • Structured, citation data	• Bibliometric analysis	Emergency preparedness and responses
17	Chatterbot for terrorism information	• Open source • Structured data	• Dialog system	Emergency preparedness and responses

For more details about case studies described above, readers are referred to:

- E. Reid and H. Chen, "Contemporary Terrorism Researchers' Patterns of Collaboration and Influence," *Journal of the American Society for Information Science and Technology*, forthcoming, 2005.

- E. Reid, J. Qin, W. Chung, J. Xu, Y. Zhou, R. Schumaker, M. Sageman, and H. Chen, "Terrorism Knowledge Discovery Project: A Knowledge Discovery Approach to Addressing the Threats of Terrorism," *Intelligence and Security Informatics*, Proceedings of the Second Symposium on Intelligence and Security Informatics, ISI 2004, Tucson, Arizona, June 2004, Lecture Notes in Computer Science (LNCS 3073), Springer-Verlag.

- R. Schumaker and H. Chen, "Leveraging Question Answer Technology to Address Terrorism Inquiry," *Decision Support Systems*, forthcoming, 2005.

- R. Schumaker and H. Chen, "Evaluating the Efficacy of a Terrorism Question Answer System: The TARA Project," *Communications of the ACM*, forthcoming, 2005.

- R. Schumaker, M. Ginsburg, H. Chen, and Y. Liu, "An Evaluation of the Chat and Knowledge Discovery Components of a Low-Level Dialog System: The AZ-ALICE Experiment," *Decision Support Systems*, forthcoming, 2005.

4.8 Future Directions

Over the past decade, through the generous funding support provided by the NSF, NIJ, DHS, and CIA, the University of Arizona Artificial Intelligence Lab and COPLINK Center have expanded their national security research from COPLINK to BorderSafe, Dark Web, and BioPortal. Based on a unique partnership model with local, state, and federal agencies in law enforcement (e.g., Tucson Police Department, Phoenix Police Department), homeland security (e.g., Customs and Border Protection), intelligence (e.g., DIA, CIA, and NSA), and disease informatics (e.g., New York and California Departments of Public Health) we have been able to make significant scientific advances and contributions in national security. The BorderSafe project will continue to explore ISI issues of relevance to creating "smart borders." The Dark Web project aims to archive open source terrorism information in multiple languages to support terrorism research and policy studies. The BioPortal project has begun to create an information sharing, analysis, and visualization framework for infectious diseases and bioagents. We hope to continue to contribute in ISI research in the next decade.

4.9 Questions for Discussion

1. What are some ways to achieve balance between basic and applied research in national security? How can important and emerging national security problems be identified?

2. What are some ways to identify government partners who can provide datasets and domain expertise? How can their cooperation be solicited?

3. How can academic research prototypes be turned into operational systems of use to national security agency partners? What are the efforts involved and resources needed?

Chapter 5

INTELLIGENCE AND WARNING

Chapter Overview

Although terrorism depends on surprise, terrorist attacks are not random but require careful planning, preparation, and cooperation before execution. To avoid being preempted by authorities, terrorists may disguise their true identities or hide their activities with their illegal objectives and intents behind other legal activities. Similarly, criminals may try to minimize the possibility of being identified and captured by using falsified identities. To detect the hidden intents and potential for future attacks or offenses is the main goal of intelligence and warning systems. In this section we present four case studies addressing the intelligence and warning needs.

5.1   Case Study 1: Detecting Deceptive Criminal Identities

It is a common practice for criminals to lie about the particulars of their identity, such as name, date of birth, address, and social security number, in order to deceive a police investigator. The ability to validate identity can be used as a warning mechanism as the deception signals the intent to commit future offenses. In this case study we focus on uncovering patterns of criminal identity deception based on actual criminal records and suggest an algorithmic approach to revealing deceptive identities (Wang et al., 2004a).

Data used in this study were authoritative criminal identity records obtained from the Tucson Police Department (TPD). These records were structured database entries containing criminal identity information, such as name, date of birth (DOB), address, identification number (e.g., social security number), race, weight, and height. Over 1.3 million criminal identity records were stored in the TPD databases. In order to study the patterns of criminal identity deception, we selected from the TPD database 372 records involving 24 criminals -- each having one real identity record and several deceptive records. Guided by a veteran police detective with over 30 years of service in law enforcement, we carefully examined these 372 records and found that deception mostly occurred in specific attributes: name, address, birth date, and ID number. The identity deception patterns in this dataset are shown in Figure 5-1.

Name deception, occurring in most deceptive cases, includes giving a false first name and a true last name or vice versa, changing the middle initial, giving a name pronounced similarly but spelled differently, etc. Deception on DOB can consist of, for example, switching places between the month of birth and the day of birth. Similarly, ID deception is often made by changing a few digits of a social security number or by switching their places. In residency deception, criminals usually change only one portion of the address. For example, we found that in about 87% of cases criminals provided a false street number along with the true street direction, street name, or street type.

To automatically detect deceptive identity records, we employed a similarity-based association mining method to extract associated (similar) record pairs. Based on the deception patterns found we selected four attributes, name, DOB, SSN, and address, for our analysis. We compared and calculated the similarity between the values of corresponding attributes of each pair of records. If two records were significantly similar we assumed that at least one of these two records was deceptive.

Because the selected four attributes have mostly string values, we compared two attribute values based on their edit distance (Levenshtein, 1966) and Soundex code (Newcombe et al., 1959). The edit distance between two strings is the minimum number of single character insertions, deletions, and substitutions required to transform one string into the other. Soundex code represents the phonetic pattern of a string. For example, "PEARSE" and "PIERCE" are both coded as "P620." To detect both spelling and phonetic variations between two name strings, edit distance similarity and Soundex similarity were computed separately. In order to capture name exchange deception, similarities were also computed based on different sequences of first name and last name. We took the similarity value from the sequence that had the maximal value between two names. We used only edit distance to compare non-phonetic attributes of DOB, SSN, and address. Each similarity value was normalized between 0 and 1. The similarity value over all four attributes was calculated using a normalized Euclidean distance function.

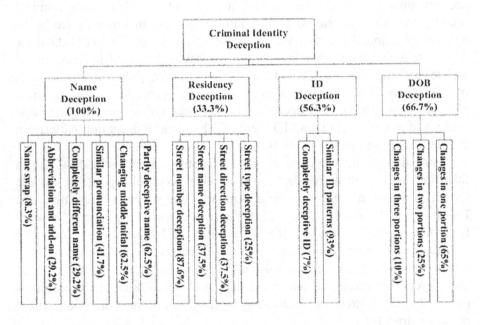

Figure 5-1. Identity deception patterns. Each percentage number represents the proportion of records that contain the particular type of deception in the selected dataset.

In order to test the performance of our approach, another sample containing 120 criminal records with identified deception was chosen from the TPD database. We ignored records with missing values. The 120 records involved 44 criminals, each of whom had an average of three records in the sample set. Some data was used to train and test our algorithm so that records pointing to the same suspect could be associated with each other. Training and testing were validated by a standard hold-out sampling method.

Of the 120 records in the testbed, 80 (2/3) were used for training the algorithm, while the remaining 40 were used for testing purposes.

A similarity matrix was built for all training records. Using the similarity values in the matrix, threshold values were searched to distinguish between the similar pairs of records and the dissimilar pairs. Accuracy rates for correctly recognized similar pairs of records using different threshold values are shown in Table 5-1. When the threshold similarity value was set to 0.52, our algorithm achieved its highest accuracy of 97.4%, with relatively small false negative and false positive rates, both of which were 2.6%.

A similarity matrix was also built for the 40 testing records. By applying the optimal threshold value to the testing similarity matrix, records having a similarity value of more than 0.52 were considered to be pointing to the same offender and were associated together. The accuracy of association in the testing dataset is shown in Table 5-2. The result shows that the algorithm is effective (with an accuracy level of 94%) in linking deceptive records pointing to the same offender.

Table 5-1. Accuracy comparison based on different threshold values.

Threshold	Accuracy	False Negative *	False Positive **
0.60	76.60%	23.40%	0.00%
0.55	92.20%	7.80%	0.00%
0.54	93.50%	6.50%	2.60%
0.53	96.10%	3.90%	2.60%
0.52	**97.40%**	**2.60%**	**2.60%**
0.51	97.40%	2.60%	6.50%
0.50	97.40%	2.60%	11.70%

* False negative: consider dissimilar records as similar ones.
** False positive: consider similar records as dissimilar ones.

Table 5-2. The accuracy of association in the testing data set.

Threshold	Accuracy	False Negative	False Positive
0.52	94.0%	6.0%	0.0%

While the above case study showed promising results, much more research is needed for deception detection, which we believe is a unique and critical problem for ISI.

5.2   Case Study 2: The Dark Web Portal

Because the Internet has become a global platform for anyone to disseminate and communicate information, terrorists also take advantage of the freedom of cyberspace and construct their own web sites to propagate terrorism beliefs, share information, and recruit new members. Web sites of terrorist organizations may also connect to one another through hyperlinks, forming a "dark web." We are building an intelligent web portal, called Dark Web Portal, to help terrorism researchers collect, access, analyze, and understand terrorist groups (Chen et al., 2004c; Reid et al., 2004). This project consists of three major components: Dark Web testbed building, Dark Web link analysis, and Dark Web Portal building.

5.2.1. Dark Web Testbed Building

Relying on reliable governmental sources such as the Anti-Defamation League (ADL), FBI, and United States Committee for a Free Lebanon (USCFL), we identified 224 U.S. domestic terrorist groups and 440 international terrorist groups. For U.S. domestic groups, group-generated URLs can be found in FBI reports and the Google Directory. For international groups, we used the group names as queries to search major search engines such as Google and manually identified the group-created URLs from the result lists. To ensure that our testbed covered major regions in the world, we sought the assistance of language experts in English, Arabic, and Spanish to help us collect URLs in several major regions. All URLs collected were manually checked by experts to make sure that they were created by terrorist groups. After the URL of a group was identified, we used the SpidersRUs toolkit, a multilingual digital library building tool developed by our lab, to collect all the web pages under that URL and store them in our testbed. Table 5-3 shows a summary of web pages collected from three rounds of spidering (performed bi-monthly).

5.2.2. Dark Web Link Analysis and Visualization

Terrorist groups are not atomized individuals but actors linked to each other through complex networks of direct or mediated exchanges. Identifying how relationships between groups are formed and dissolved in the terrorist group network would enable us to decipher the social milieu and communication channels among terrorist groups across different jurisdictions. Previous studies have shown that the link structure of the web represents a considerable amount of latent human annotation (Gibson et al., 1998). Thus, by analyzing and visualizing hyperlink structures between terrorist-generated web sites and their content, we could discover the structure and organization of terrorist group networks, capture network dynamics, and understand their emerging activities.

Table 5-3. Summary of URLs identified and web pages collected.

Region		U.S.A. Domestic			Latin-America			Middle-East		
Batch #		1st	2nd	3rd	1st	2nd	3rd	1st	2nd	3rd
# of seed URLs	Total	81	233	108	37	83	68	69	128	135
	From literature & reports	63	113	58	0	0	0	23	31	37
	From search engines	0	0	0	37	48	41	46	66	66
	From link extraction	18	120	50	0	32	27	0	31	32
# of terrorist groups searched		74	219	71	7	10	10	34	36	36
# of Web pages	Total	125,610	396,105	746,297	106,459	332,134	394,315	322,524	222,687	1,004,785
	Multi-media files	0	70,832	223,319	0	44,671	83,907	0	35,164	83,907

5.2.3. Dark Web Portal Building

Using the Dark Web Portal, users are able to quickly locate specific dark web information in the testbed through keyword search. To address the information overload problem, the Dark Web Portal is designed with post-retrieval components. A modified version of a text summarizer called TXTRACTOR, which uses sentence-selection heuristics to rank and select important text segments (McDonald and Chen, 2002), has been added into the Dark Web Portal. The summarizer can flexibly summarize web pages using three or five sentences, so that users can quickly get the main idea of a web page without having to read though it. A categorizer organizes the search results into various folders labeled by the key phrases extracted by the Arizona Noun Phraser (AZNP) (Tolle and Chen, 2000) from the page summaries or titles, thereby facilitating the understanding of different groups of web pages. A visualizer clusters web pages into colored regions using the Kohonen self-organizing map (SOM) algorithm (Kohonen, 1995), thus reducing the information overload problem when a large number of search results are obtained. Post-retrieval analysis could help reduce the information overload problem. However, without addressing the language barrier problem, researchers are limited to the data in their native languages and cannot fully utilize the multilingual information in our testbed. To address this problem, we added a cross-lingual information retrieval (CLIR) component into the portal. Based on our previous research, we have developed a dictionary-based CLIR system for use in the Dark Web Portal. It currently accepts English queries and retrieves documents in English, Spanish, Chinese, and Arabic. Another component that will be added to the Dark Web Portal is a machine translation (MT) component, which will translate the multilingual information retrieved by the CLIR component back into the users' native languages.

We show a sample search session in the figures below. Suppose the user is interested in the terrorist group "Ku Klux Klan" and uses it as a search term. Two types of search forms are available: simple search and advanced search (see Figure 5-2). Our user chose to use the simple search first. The advanced mode gives users more options to refine their search. For example, the user can specify web pages with the exact phrase. In addition, the user can restrict the results within a few terrorist categories or choose to search a particular file type, such as PDF or Word files.

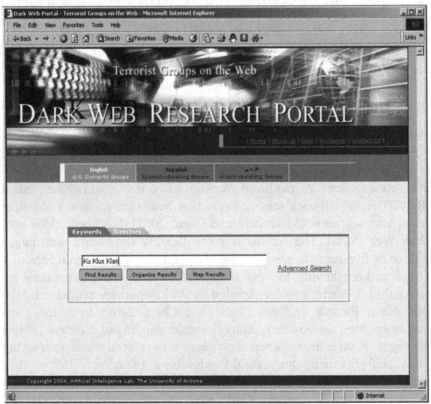

Figure 5-2. Dark Web Portal interfaces: simple search and advanced search.
Figure 5-2a. U.S. domestic (English) simple search interface.

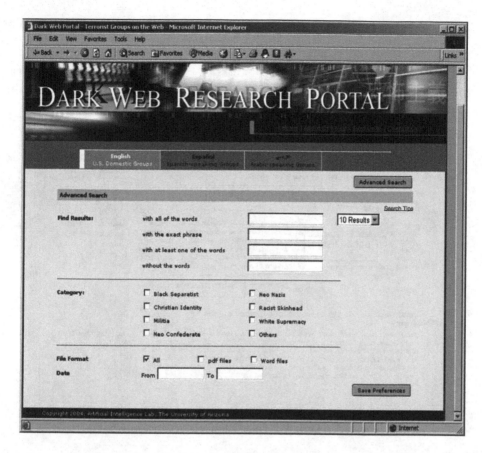

Figure 5-2b. U.S. domestic (English) advanced search interface.

By hitting the "Find Results" button, the top 20 results are displayed (see Figure 5-3). On the top of the result page it shows a list of "suggested keywords," such as "Aryan Nations" and "David Duke," which helps the user to expand or refine the query. Along with the web page result display, our portal also presents the terrorist group name and the corresponding group category. As terrorist group web pages may often disappear, "Cached Pages" for each web page collected at different time periods are provided (e.g., 2004/03). Additionally, the user can view web pages, PDF files, or Word files by clicking the corresponding links.

As terrorist groups continue to use the Internet as their communication, recruiting, and propaganda tool, a systematic and system-aided approach to studying their presence on the web is critically needed.

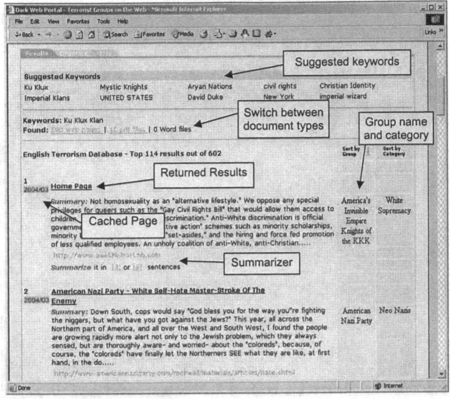

Figure 5-3. Dark Web Portal interfaces: returned results.

5.3   Case Study 3: Jihad on the Web

With weekly news coverage of excerpts from videos produced and web cast by terrorists, it has become clear that terrorists have further exploited the Internet beyond routine communication and propaganda operations to better influence the outside world (Arquilla & Rondeldt, 1996). Some terrorism researchers posited that terrorists have used the Internet as a broadcast platform for the "terrorist news network," which is an effective tactic because they can reach a broad audience with relatively little chance of detection (Elison, 2000; Tsfati & Weimann, 2002; Weinmann, 2004). Although this alternate side of the Internet, referred to as the "Dark Web," has recently received extensive government and media attention, systematic understanding of how terrorists use the Internet for their campaign of terror is very limited.

In this study, we explore an integrated computer-based approach to harvesting and analyzing web sites produced or maintained by Islamic Jihad extremist groups or their sympathizers to deepen our understanding of how

Jihad terrorists use the Internet, especially the World Wide Web, in their terror campaigns. More specifically, we built a high-quality Jihad terrorism web collection using a web harvesting approach and conducted hyperlink analysis on this collection to reveal various facets of Jihad terrorism web usage. We hope to supplement existing high-quality but manually-driven terrorism research with a systematic, automated web spidering and mining methodology.

5.3.1. Building the Jihad Web Collection

To guarantee that our collection is comprehensive and representative, we take a three-step systematic approach to construct our collection:

1. *Identifying seed URLs and backlink expansion*: The first task is to find a small set of high-quality Jihad web sites. To identify terrorist groups, we completely relied on the U.S. Department of State's list of foreign terrorist organizations. In particular, we only selected Middle-Eastern organizations from that list for this study. After identifying the terrorist groups in the Middle-East region, we manually searched major search engines to find the web sites of these groups. Our goal was not to construct a comprehensive list of URLs, but merely to compile a small list of high-quality URLs that can serve as the seeds for backlink expansion. The backlinks of these URLs were automatically identified through Google and Yahoo backline search services and a collection of 88 web sites was automatically retrieved.

2. *Manual collection filtering*: Because bogus or unrelated terrorist sites can make their way into our collection, we developed a manual filtering process based on evidence and clues in the web sites. Aside from sites which explicitly identify themselves as the official sites of a terrorist organization or one of its members, a web site that contains praise of or adopts ideologies espoused by a terrorist group is included in our collection.

3. *Extending search*: To ensure the comprehensiveness of our collection we augment the collection by means of expanded searches. Based on the 26 web sites identified in the previous step, we constructed a small lexicon of commonly-used Jihad terms with the help of Arabic language speakers. Examples of highly relevant keywords included in the lexicon are: "حرب صليبية" ("Crusader's War"), "المجاهدين" ("Moujahedin"), "الكفار" ("Infidels"), etc. This lexicon is utilized to perform expanded searches. The same rules used in the filtering process are used here to discern fake and unrelated web sites. As a result, our final Jihad web collection

contains 109,477 Jihad web documents including HTML pages, plain text files, PDF documents, and Microsoft Word documents.

5.3.2. Hyperlink Analysis on the Jihad Web Collection

We believe the exploration of hidden Jihad web communities can give insight into the nature of real-world relationships and communication channels between terrorist groups (Weimann, 2004). Uncovering hidden web communities involves calculating a similarity measure between all pairs of web sites in our collection. We define similarity as a function of the number of hyperlinks in web site "A" that point to web site "B," and vice versa. In addition, a hyperlink is weighted proportionally to how deep it appears in the web site hierarchy. The similarity matrix is then used as input to a Multi-Dimensional Scaling (MDS) algorithm (Torgerson, 1952), which generates a two dimensional graph of the web sites. The proximity of nodes in the graph reflects their similarity level.

As shown in Figure 5-4, domain experts recognized six clusters representing hyperlinked communities in the network. On the left side of the network resides the Hizbollah cluster. Hizbollah is a Lebanese militant organization. Established in 1982 during the Israeli invasion of Lebanon, the group routinely attacked Israeli military personnel until their pullout from south Lebanon in 2000. A cluster of web sites of Palestinian organizations occupies the bottom-left corner of the network, including: Hamas, Al-Aqsa Martyr's Brigades, and the Palestinian Islamic Jihad. An interesting observation here is the close link between the Hizbollah community and the Palestinian militant groups' community. Hizbollah has traditionally sympathized with the Palestinian cause.

On the top-left corner sits the Hizb-ut-Tahrir cluster. Hizb-ut-Tahrir is a political party with branches in many countries in the Middle-East and in Europe. Although the group is believed to be associated with Al-Qaeda, an apparent relationship between the two groups has not been proven. Looking at the bottom-right corner, one can see a cluster of Al-Qaeda affiliated sites. This cluster has links to two radical Palestinian web sites. Al-Qaeda sympathizes with Palestinian groups and some Palestinian Islamist groups like Hamas and Islamic Jihad share the same Salafi ideology with Al-Qaeda. In the top-right corner, the Jihad Sympathizers web community includes web sites maintained by sympathizers of the Global Salafi movement. For example, "kavkazcenter.net" and "clearguidance.com" are two web sites maintained by sympathizers of the Chechen rebels. As expected, the sympathizers' community does not have any links to Hizbollah's community as they follow radically different ideologies.

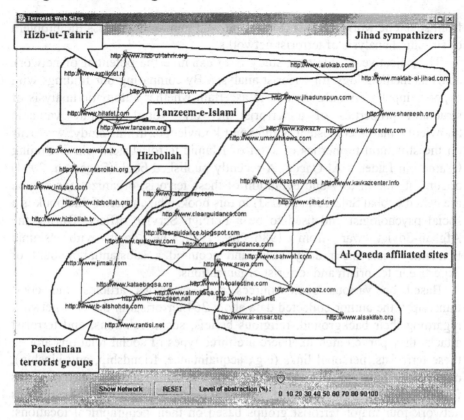

Figure 5-4. The Jihad terrorism web site network visualized based on hyperlinks.

Visualizing hyperlinked communities can lead to a better understanding of the Jihad web presence. Furthermore, it helps foretell likely relationships between terrorist groups.

5.4 Case Study 4: Analyzing the Al-Qaeda Network

As part of the worldwide Islamic revivalist movement, a number of terrorist organizations have targeted the West. Terrorism and terrorist attacks pose severe threats and have brought significant damage to the whole world. Only with an in-depth understanding of terrorism and terrorist organizations can we defend against the threats. Because terrorist organizations often operate in a network form in which individual terrorists cooperate and collaborate with each other to carry out attacks (Klerks, 2001; Krebs, 2001), network analysis methodology can help discover valuable knowledge about terrorist organizations by studying the structural properties of the networks (Xu and Chen, Forthcoming). We have employed techniques and methods from social network analysis (SNA) and web mining to address the problem of structural analysis of terrorist networks.

The objective of this case study is to examine the potential of network analysis methodology for terrorist analysis. By comparing our findings with experts' input we would be able to ascertain whether automatic analysis of structural properties of a terrorist network would generate valuable knowledge that is consistent with expert knowledge. In this study, we focus on the structural properties of a set of Islamic terrorist networks including Osama bin Laden's Al-Qaeda. A recently published book (Sageman, 2004) documents the history and evolution of these terrorist organizations, which are called Global Salafi Jihad (GSJ) in this book. The author of this book is a social psychologist and used to be a Foreign Service officer. During the Afghan-Soviet war from 1986 to 1989, he dealt with Islamic Fundamentalists on a daily basis and acquired a substantial amount of expertise in terrorism and terrorist organizations.

Based on various open sources such as news articles and court transcripts, the author collected data about 364 terrorists in the GSJ network regarding their background, religious beliefs, social relations, and terrorist attacks they participated in. There are three types of social relations among these terrorists: personal links (e.g., acquaintance, friendship, and kinship), operational links (e.g., collaborators in the same attack), and relations formed after attacks (Sageman, 2004). The author identified within this network four major terrorist groups based on their geographical locations: Central Staff, Core Arab, Maghreb Arab, and Southeast Asian. Each group has its own leaders. For example, Osama bin Laden is the leader of the Core Staff group, which connects to the other three groups through several lieutenants.

We analyzed the GSJ network based on the social relation data contained in a spreadsheet provided by the author. Using the SNA visualization approach we depicted the GSJ network graphically as shown in Figure 5-5.

- *Centrality analysis.* Considering all three types of social relations, we found that the four group leaders were among the top 11 most popular members, where the popularity was represented by degree measure. For example, Osama bin Laden had 72 links to other terrorists and ranked the second in degree. Although he was not a leader, Hambali had the highest degree score and played an important role in connecting different terrorist groups (see Figure 5-5a). Moreover, the lieutenants tended to have high scores in betweenness and served as gatekeepers between groups. The analysis implies that centrality measures could be useful for identifying important members in a terrorist network.

- *Subgroup analysis*. The four terrorist groups are shown in Figure 5-5b, based on the author's input. To find out whether these geographical-based groups were also cohesive groups in structure, we calculated the cohesion score (Wasserman and Faust, 1994) of each group. We found that all these groups had high cohesion scores. The Southeast Asian group scored the highest in cohesion. This may suggest that members in this group tended to be more closely related to members in their own group than to members from other groups. According to the author, the Southeast Asian group was quite different from the other three groups in terms of their religious beliefs and missions.

- *Network structure analysis*. According to the author, these groups had different structures: the Southeast Asian group's structure was hierarchical, in which members at higher levels lead lower-level members, while the other three groups were scale-free networks (Albert and Barabasi, 2002). However, we found that the four groups were similar in their degree distribution, which was a power-law distribution with a long tail for large values of degree. This implies that all four networks were scale-free networks in which a few important members (nodes with high degree scores) dominated the network and new members tend to join a network through these dominating members. This finding has an important policy implication, that is, disruptive strategies should potentially be focused on central members in a terrorist network.

- *Link path analysis*. Comparing the personal network representation (Figure 5-5b) and the operational network representation (Figure 5-5c), we found that some important members did not have direct personal links to an attack prior to the execution of the attack. For example, Osama bin Laden, KSM, and Hambali had no direct personal links to terrorists in the 9/11 attack clique. We performed link path analysis to find out the shortest paths of personal links that lead to 9/11 terrorists. One of our hypotheses was that Osama bin Laden connected to the 9/11 clique through a four-hop path: bin Laden – Nashiri – ZaMihd – Mihdhar – Shibh (the highlighted path in Figure 5-5b). Although this hypothesis turned out to be wrong based on the author's feedback (other information was needed to establish the link), the analysis showed the potential of using link path analysis to generate hypotheses about the motives and planning processes of terrorist attacks.

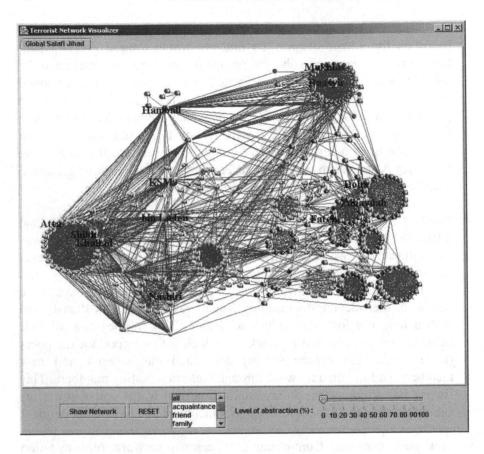

Figure 5-5. The Global Salafi Jihad (GSJ) network.
Figure 5-5a. The GSJ network with all types of relations. Each node represents a terrorist. A link represents a social relation. The four terrorist groups are color-coded in original figures (not shown here): Central Staff—pink, Core Arab—yellow, Maghreb Arab—blue, and Southeast Asian—green. Leaders are labeled in red and lieutenants are labeled in black.

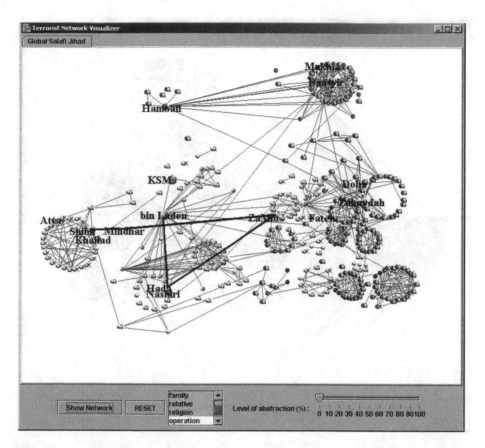

Figure 5-5b. The GSJ network with personal links. The highlighted path indicates the hypothesis regarding the connection between bin Laden and the 9/11 attacks.

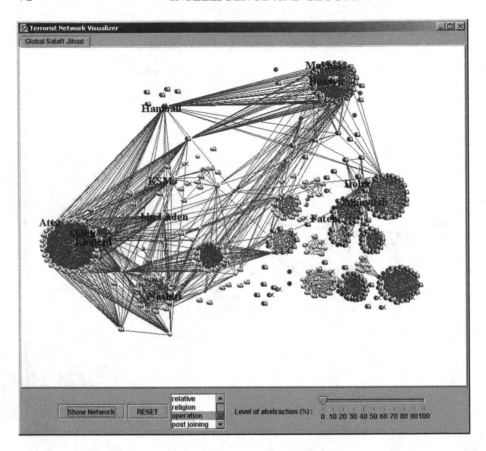

Figure 5-5c. The GSJ network with operational links. A link between two terrorists indicates that they were involved in the same attack. The circles can also be called cliques where group members are densely connected with other members.

5.5   Future Directions

Deception detection is one of the unique problems facing law enforcement and intelligence applications. Criminals and terrorists often try to hide or disguise their identities via various means. Biometric (e.g., fingerprints and DNA) techniques and behavioral or psychological interrogations have been widely adopted in law enforcement and intelligence communities. With the abundance of criminal identity information available in law enforcement and intelligence databases and the ability of advanced algorithms for "fuzzy" queries and entity matching, we believe data mining guided deception detection research shows tremendous potential.

We also believe that web-based open source "terrorism informatics" research is critically needed for terrorism research and intelligence analysis purposes. There is a pressing need for traditional terrorism researchers and analysts to leverage the new advances in web retrieval, mining, analysis, and visualization. By combining the domain expertise and methodology well established in terrorism research with new information technologies, we believe the new science of terrorism informatics would emerge and contribute to the systematic study and understanding of the global terrorism phenomena.

5.6   Questions for Discussion

1. What are other deception detection applications in the law enforcement or intelligence community? How can relevant datasets be obtained?

2. What are some ways to identify terrorism researchers? What are the major terrorism research conferences and publications? What are the major terrorism research centers?

3. What are some ways to collaborate with the intelligence community for non-security clearance level research? What are some of the rich open sources for technical ISI research?

4. What are some ways to develop and advance multilingual and multimedia research in ISI? What are the technical foundations and promising approaches?

Chapter 6

BORDER AND TRANSPORTATION SECURITY

Chapter Overview

Terrorists enter a targeted country through an air, land, or sea port of entry. Criminals in narcotics rings travel across borders to purchase, carry, distribute, and sell drugs. Creating a "smart border" can greatly improve the government's counter-terrorism and crime-fighting capabilities, where information from borders, customs, departments of transportation, and local law enforcement are integrated and analyzed to help locate terrorists or criminals. We present our "BorderSafe" project for cross-jurisdictional information sharing and criminal network analysis as an example for creating a smart and safe border.

6.1 Case Study 5: Enhancing "BorderSafe" Information Sharing

The BorderSafe project is a collaborative research effort involving the University of Arizona's Artificial Intelligence Lab, law enforcement agencies, including the Tucson Police Department (TPD), Pima County Sheriff's Department (PCSD), and Tucson Customs and Border Protection (CBP), as well as San Diego ARJIS (Automated Regional Justice Information Systems, a regional consortium of 50+ public safety agencies), San Diego Supercomputer Center (SDSC), and the Corporation for National Research Initiative (CNRI).

In this study our objective was to share and analyze structured, authoritative data from TPD, PCSD, and a limited dataset from CBP containing license plate data of border crossing vehicles. Tables 6-1 and 6-2 present the statistics of the three datasets. TPD's and PCSD's jurisdictions represent a shared community of citizens in Tucson and southern Arizona. They also share intertwined communities of criminals in these areas. We found a substantial amount of data overlap among these datasets. Around 7% of vehicles involved in gang-related, violent, and narcotics crimes were registered outside of Arizona. More than 483,000 people appeared in both the TPD and PCSD datasets. That represented 36% of the TPD records and 37% of the PCSD records. These statistics strongly suggest that sharing information across jurisdictions could help catch criminals.

Table 6-1. Statistics regarding the TPD and PCSD datasets.

	TPD	PCSD
Number of recorded incidents	2.84 million	2.18 million
Number of persons	1.35 million	1.31 million
Number of vehicles	62,656	520,539

Table 6-2. CBP border crossing dataset.

Item	Number
Number of records	1,125,155
Number of distinct vehicles	226,207
Number of plates issued in AZ	130,195
Number of plates issued in CA	5,546
Number of plates issued in Mexico	90,466

We employed the federation approach for data integration. At the schema level, we adopted the COPLINK schema as the global schema and developed a transformation mechanism to reconcile the database structure and semantics from a particular database into the global schema. Data were then mapped or transformed to allow shared query processing. In our datasets, the establishment of automated transformation procedures for putting legacy PCSD and TPD records into COPLINK format resolved most structural and semantic difference issues.

At the instance level, each dataset had a unique key assigned to each person or vehicle, but these unique keys did not match across datasets. To address this problem, vehicles were then matched between datasets based on their license plate numbers.

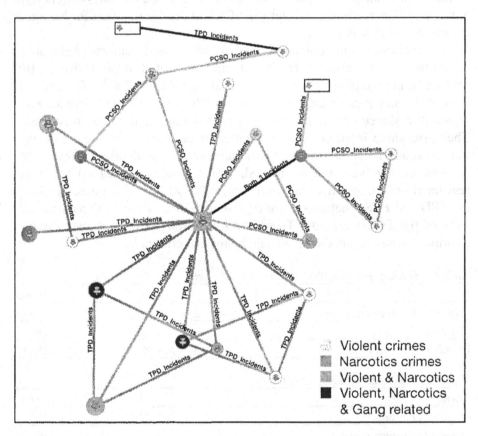

Figure 6-1. A sample criminal network based on integrated data from multiple sources. (In original figures, border crossing plates are outlined in red. Associations found in the TPD data are blue, PCSD links are green, and when a link is found in both sets the link is colored red. Colors are not shown here.)

For people match, we based the matching on input from domain experts and assumed that all records with the same first name, last name, and DOB represented the same person. These heuristics were not perfect; a few incorrect matches resulted and certainly many correct matches might have been missed.

We generated and visualized several criminal networks based on integrated data. We extracted associations between a set of criminals and vehicles from crime incident records. A link was created when two or more criminals or vehicles were listed in the same incident record. In network visualization we differentiated entity types by shape, key attributes by node color, level of activeness (measured by number of crimes committed) as node size, data source by link color, and some details in link text or roll-over tool tips. Figure 6-1 shows a network connecting a known narcotics dealer to a border crossing license plate.

A qualitative field study was conducted to assess the potential of our data integration approach. We received positive feedback regarding the value of integrated data. The crime analysts who participated in the evaluation study expressed confidence that including border crossing information into their investigations would promptly result in arrests and convictions. One analyst commented: "I had no idea that these types of complex networks involving Mexican plates even existed in the Tucson area. That information could subsequently be used to focus and direct law enforcement resources and investigations."

6.2 Case Study 6: Topological Analysis of Cross-Jurisdictional Criminal Networks

A criminal activity network (CAN) is a network of interconnected criminals, vehicles, and locations based on law enforcement records. The networks can be augmented with data from sources like transportation systems and motor vehicle division data. These networks allow us to analyze and visualize information that is helpful for identifying suspicious vehicles and people at the border or around critical infrastructures. Criminal activity networks can contain information from multiple sources and be used to identify relationships between people and vehicles that are unknown to a single jurisdiction (Chen et al., 2004). As a result, cross-jurisdictional information sharing and triangulation can help generate better investigative leads and strengthen legal cases against criminals.

Criminal activity networks can be large and complex (particularly in a cross-jurisdictional environment) and can be better analyzed if we study their topological properties. Topological properties describe the network as a whole and help us better understand its governing mechanisms. Topological properties can also be used to quantify the advantages of data sharing to law enforcement and transportation security agencies/personnel. In addition, understanding the properties of CANs can help design better analysis tools to assist in identifying potentially dangerous vehicles and people. In this study, we examine the topological properties of, and explore important research questions related to, cross-jurisdictional criminal activity networks.

Complex networks of individuals and other entities have been traditionally studied under the random graph theory. However, later studies suggested that real-world complex networks may not be random but may be governed by certain organizing principles (Albert & Barabasi, 2002). This prompted the study of real-world networks. These studies have explored the topology, evolution and growth, robustness and attack tolerance, and other properties of networks.

The datasets used in this study are available to us through the DHS-funded BorderSafe project. To study criminal activity networks we used police incident reports from the Tucson Police Department (TPD) and the Pima County Sheriff's Department (PCSD) from 1990 – 2002.

This testbed was used to extract narcotics networks that consisted of vehicles and individuals as nodes and police incidents as edges between them. Individuals were included as nodes in the network if they were wanted, suspected, arrested, or had a warrant for arrest in a narcotics crime. Vehicles were included as nodes in the network if they had been involved with a suspect in a narcotics crime. Two nodes were connected by an edge if they were in the same incident involving a narcotics or narcotics-related crime. Table 6-3 presents the basic statistics of the narcotics networks extracted from TPD and PCSD's records.

A giant component containing the majority of the nodes emerges from both networks. This is not uncommon; other social and affiliation networks that have been studied before exhibit this structure. The giant component, in this case, is a large group of individuals linked by narcotics crimes. In addition, we find that the second largest component is significantly smaller, suggesting that other much smaller groups of people exist in both jurisdictions.

Table 6-3. Basic statistics of TPD and PCSD narcotics networks.

	TPD	PCSD
Nodes	31,478 individuals	11,173 individuals
Edges	82,696	67,106
Giant component	22,393 (70%)	10,610 (94%)
2nd largest component	41	103
Associated border crossing vehicles	6,927	2,979

Table 6-4. Small world properties of narcotics networks. Values in parenthesis are values for a random network of the same size and average degree.

	TPD	PCSD
Clustering Coefficient	0.39 (1.39 x 10⁻⁴)	0.53 (4.08 x 10⁻⁴)
Average Shortest Path Length (L)	5.09 (8.80)	4.62 (6.32)
Diameter	22	23

The small-world and scale-free properties of these and other networks shown later are studied by using the giant component. The small-world properties of both networks are shown in Table 6-4.

The narcotics networks in both jurisdictions can be classified as small-world networks since their clustering coefficients are much higher than comparable random graphs, and they have a small average shortest path length (L) relative to their size. The high clustering coefficient suggests that criminals show a tendency to form circles of associates who partner in crimes. According to domain experts this is not unusual in narcotics networks, where individuals tend to have circles of trust that include friends and family members. This property is advantageous to law enforcement because it helps them form strong conspiracy cases against other members of the group. A small L implies a faster flow of information (e.g., news of police raids) and goods (e.g., drugs) in the network. However, short paths could be advantageous for law enforcement too. Investigators search for associations among criminals to form a case against them. They suggest that shorter association paths between criminals generate better and higher quality investigative leads. Table 6-5 presents the scale-free properties of both networks.

Table 6-5. Scale free properties of narcotics networks.

	TPD	PCSD
Average Degree, <k> (average number of partners in crime)	3.12	4.33
Maximum Degree (largest number of partners in crime)	84	96
Exponent, γ	1.3	0.85
Cutoff, κ	17.24	16.71

The narcotics networks have degree distributions that follow the truncated power law, which classifies them as scale-free networks. This implies that a large number of nodes have low degrees as shown by the slow rate of decay (exponents of $0.85 - 1.3$) at low values of k. This is not unexpected since high degrees attract more attention from law enforcement authorities, so having fewer associates is beneficial. However, it is worth pointing out that the degree of a node in these narcotics networks is also restricted by the fact that we are considering only narcotics-related crimes (to extract 'pure' narcotics networks). If other common crimes like traffic citations are included, then degrees are likely to be greater. Thus, the exponent (γ) value can be affected by the methods used for network extraction. The truncated power law distribution fits both curves better ($R^2 = 93\%$) than the power law distribution ($R^2 = 85\%$, 87%). This suggests that as the degree (k) increases, the probability of having k links ($p(k)$) decreases. This might indicate a cost or trust constraint to growth.

Table 6-6 shows the topological properties of the TPD narcotics network when it is augmented with associations found in PCSD data. No additional individuals from PCSD data were added.

Table 6-6. Topological statistics on adding associations (found in PCSD data) between the individuals in the TPD narcotics network. Values in parenthesis are for the original TPD network.

Giant component	27,700 (22,393)
Edges	98,763 (70,079)
Associated border crossing vehicles	8,975 (6,927)
Clustering coefficient	0.36 (0.39)
Average Shortest Path Length (L)	8.54 (5.09)
Diameter	24 (22)
Average degree, <k>	3.56 (3.12)
Maximum degree	96 (84)
Exponent, γ	1.01 (1.3)
Cutoff, κ	16.39 (17.24)

In Table 6-6, we see that the size of the giant component in the TPD narcotics network increases. Nodes that were previously thought to be disconnected from the main network got connected. Since we added only associations, it is clear that PCSD data contained associations between individuals in TPD data that TPD was not aware of. The increase in the number of edges shows that previously unknown associations between existing and new nodes were added. From a total of 28,684 new relationships added, 6,300 (statistic not in Table 6-6) were between existing criminals in the TPD narcotics network. These new associations between existing people help form a stronger case against criminals. The increase in the number of nodes and associations is a convincing example of the advantage of sharing data between jurisdictions.

The topological properties have important implications for law enforcement and hence transportation security. We found that a single jurisdiction may contain incomplete information on criminals and cross-jurisdictional data provides an increased number of high-quality investigative leads. The inclusion of vehicular data in criminal activity networks had clear advantages. Vehicles provided new investigative leads that can be used to target individuals and vehicles that might pose a threat to the security of the border and transportation infrastructure.

6.3 Future Directions

Many federal agencies are directly involved in protecting the safety of the U.S. borders (e.g., Immigration, Customs and Border Protection, Transportation Security Agency, Border Patrols, etc). Although most of these previously disparate agencies are consolidated under the Department of Homeland Security, significant cultural, organizational, and information technology barriers exist. In addition, other federal agencies, such as the FBI and the CIA, and local jurisdictions also hold critical information about selected border crossers and vehicles that may be of relevance. With the passage of the USA PATRIOT Act and the continuous re-structuring within DHS, we hope to see a more cooperative relationship among these agencies for information sharing.

However, information sharing without careful data mining research or civil liberties considerations will only cause information overload and potential misuse. Unreasonable border protection and immigration policy could also severely affect international trading. Much policy and technical research is needed for border and transportation security in this era of increasing globalization.

6.4 Questions for Discussion

1. How can information technology research and civil liberties considerations be balanced in the context of border and transportation security?

2. What are some ways to collaborate with various DHS agencies in border and transportation security research? What are the relevant DHS funding programs?

3. What are some of the other relevant technologies and techniques for border and transportation security research?

Chapter 7

DOMESTIC COUNTER-TERRORISM

Chapter Overview

As terrorists may be involved in local crimes, state and local law enforcement agencies are contributing to national security by investigating and prosecuting crimes. Terrorism, like gangs and narcotics trafficking, is treated as a type of organized crime in which multiple offenders cooperate to carry out offenses. Information technologies that help find cooperative relationships between criminals and their interactive patterns would also be helpful in analyzing terrorism. Through three case studies in this section, we show how criminal association information can be extracted from large volumes of data and how structural patterns in criminal or terrorist organizations can be discovered.

7.1   Case Study 7: COPLINK Detect

Crime analysts and detectives search for criminal associations to develop investigative leads. However, because association information is not directly available in most existing law enforcement and intelligence databases and manual searching is extremely time-consuming, automatic identification of relationships among criminal entities may significantly speed up crime investigations. COPLINK Detect is a system that automatically extracts criminal element relationships from large volumes of crime incident data (Hauck et al., 2002).

Our data were structured crime incident records stored in TPD databases. TPD's current record management system (RMS) consists of more than 1.5 million crime incident records that contain details from criminal events spanning the period from 1986 to 2004. Although investigators can access the RMS to tie together information, they must manually search the RMS for connections or existing relationships.

We used the concept space approach (Chen and Lynch, 1992) to identify relationships between entities of interest. Concept space analysis is a type of co-occurrence analysis used in information retrieval. The resulting network-like concept space holds all possible associations between terms, which means that the system retains and ranks every existing link between every pair of concepts. In COPLINK Detect, detailed incident records served as the underlying space, while concepts derive from the meaningful terms that occur in each incident. Concept space analysis easily identifies relevant terms and their degree of relationship to the search term. The system output includes relevant terms ranked in the order of their degree of association, thereby distinguishing the most relevant terms from inconsequential terms. From a crime investigation standpoint, concept space analysis can help investigators link known entities to other related entities that might contain useful information for further investigation, such as people and vehicles related to a given suspect. It is considered an example of entity association mining (Lin and Brown, 2003).

Information related to a suspect can direct an investigation to expand in the right direction, but revealing relationships among data in one particular incident might fail to capture those relationships from the entire database. In effect, investigators need to review all incident reports related to a suspect, which can be tedious work. The COPLINK Detect system introduces concept space as an alternative method that captures the relationships between four types of entities (person, organization, location, and vehicle) in the entire database. COPLINK Detect also offers an easy-to-use user interface and allows searching for relationships among the four types of entities.

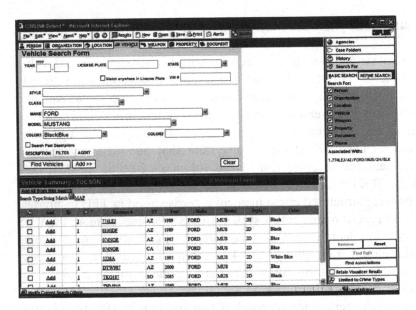

Figure 7-1. COPLINK Detect interface showing sample research results.

Figure 7-1a. COPLINK Detect vehicle search screen. "Vehicle" is one of the information types users can enter as a search term. After adding the search terms to the Associated With box, the user selects the Find Associations button to retrieve associates.

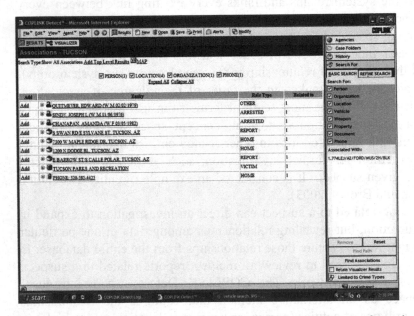

Figure 7-1b. Associations screen. The application can return elements for each of the eight information object types: Person, Organization, Location, Vehicle, Weapon, Property, Document, and Phone. Here the search has return results for three persons, four locations, one organization, and one phone number.

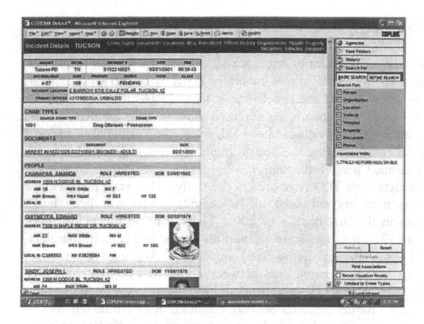

Figure 7-1c. Incident Details screen. In this example, the detective can view the details of one prior incident in the database, including the role and home address of each person involved. (All criminal data shown here are scrubbed.)

Figure 7-1 presents the COPLINK Detect interface showing sample search results of vehicles, relations, and crime case details (Hauck et al., 2002).

We conducted user studies to evaluate the performance and usefulness of COPLINK Detect. Twelve crime analysts and detectives participated in the field study during a four-week period. Three major areas were identified where COPLINK Detect provided improved support for crime investigation:

- *Link analysis*. Participants indicated that COPLINK Detect served as a powerful tool for acquiring criminal association information. They cited its value in helping determine the presence or absence of links between people, places, vehicles, and other entity types in investigating a crime.

- *Interface design*. In general, users reported that they found the COPLINK Detect interface easy to use. Officers noted that the graphical user interface and use of color to distinguish different entity types provided a more intuitive visualization than traditional text-based record management systems.

- *Operating efficiency*. In a direct comparison of 15 searches, using COPLINK Detect required an average of 30 minutes less per search than did a benchmark record management system (20 minutes vs. 50 minutes).

7.2   Case Study 8: Criminal Network Mining

Because organized crimes are carried out by networked offenders, investigation of organized crimes naturally depends on network analysis approaches. Grounded on social network analysis (SNA) methodology, our criminal network structure mining research aims to help intelligence and security agencies extract valuable knowledge regarding criminal or terrorist organizations by identifying the central members, subgroups, and network structure (Xu and Chen, Forthcoming).

Two datasets from TPD were used in the study. (1) A gang network: the list of gang members consisted of 16 offenders who had been under investigation in the first quarter of 2002. These gang members had been involved in 72 crime incidents of various types (e.g., theft, burglary, aggravated assault, drug offense, etc.) since 1985. We used the concept space approach and generated links between criminals who had committed crimes together, resulting in a network of 164 members. (2) A narcotics network: the list for the narcotics network consisted of 71 criminal names. A sergeant from the Gang Unit had been studying the activities of these criminals since 1995. Because most of them had committed crimes related to methamphetamines, the sergeant called this network the "Meth World." These offenders had been involved in 1,206 incidents since 1983. A network of 744 members was generated.

We employed SNA approaches to extract structural patterns in our criminal networks.

- *Network Partition.* We employed hierarchical clustering, namely the complete-link algorithm, to partition a network into subgroups based on relational strength. Clusters obtained represent subgroups. To employ the algorithm, we first transformed co-occurrence weights generated in the previous phrase into distances/dissimilarities. The distance between two clusters was defined as the distance between the pair of nodes drawn from each cluster that was farthest apart. The algorithm worked by merging the two nearest clusters into one cluster at each step and eventually formed a cluster hierarchy. The resulting cluster hierarchy specified groupings of network members at different granularity levels. At lower levels of the hierarchy, clusters (subgroups) tended to be smaller and group members were more closely related. At higher levels of the hierarchy, subgroups are large and group members might be loosely related.

- *Centrality Measures.* We used all three centrality measures to identify central members in a given subgroup. The degree of a node could be obtained by counting the total number of links it had to all the other group members. A node's score of betweenness and closeness required the computation of shortest paths (geodesics) using Dijkstra's algorithm (1959).

- *Blockmodeling.* At a given level of a cluster hierarchy, we compared between-group link densities with the network's overall link density to determine the presence or absence of between-group relationships.

- *Visualization.* To map a criminal network onto a two-dimensional display, we employed Multi-Dimensional Scaling (MDS) to generate x-y coordinates for each member in a network. We chose Torgerson's classical MDS algorithm (Torgerson, 1952) since distances transformed from co-occurrence weights were quantitative data.

A graphical user interface was provided to visualize criminal networks. Figure 7-2 shows the screenshot of our prototype system. In this example, each node was labeled with the name of the criminal it represented. Criminal names were scrubbed for data confidentiality. A straight line connecting two nodes indicated that two corresponding criminals committed crimes together and thus were related. To find subgroups and interaction patterns between groups, a user could adjust the "level of abstraction" slider at the bottom of the panel. A high level of abstraction corresponded with a high distance level in the cluster hierarchy. Group members' rankings in centrality are listed in a table.

We conducted a qualitative study recently to evaluate the prototype system. We presented the two testing networks to domain experts at TPD and received encouraging feedback:

- *Subgroups detected were mostly correct.* Our domain experts checked and validated the members in each group. These groups had different characteristics with different specialties or crime preferences. We also found that although relationships in our networks were extracted based on crime incidents, they reflected true relationships between criminals such as friendship, kinship, and even conflicts.

- *Centrality measures provided ways of identifying key members in a network.* According to our domain experts, betweenness was a reliable measure to identify gatekeepers between subgroups. However, degree sometimes identified wrong leaders because the criminals with the most connections to others may not always be the leaders. Leaders may be smart enough to hide behind other criminals to avoid police contact.

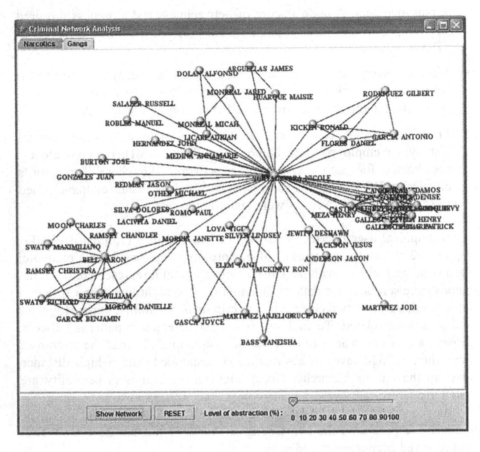

Figure 7-2. An SNA-based system for criminal network analysis and visualization.
Figure 7-2a. A 57-member criminal network. Each node is labeled using the name of the
criminal it represents. Lines represent the relationships between criminals.

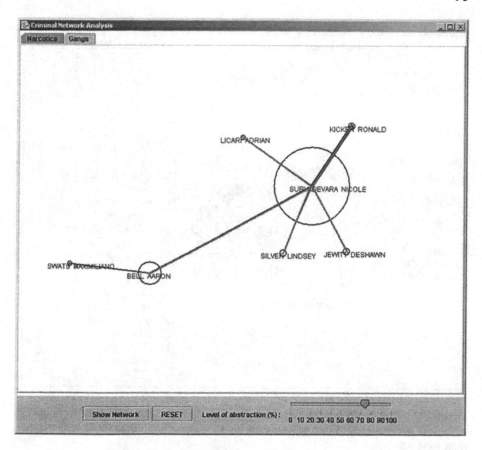

Figure 7-2b. The reduced structure of the network. Each circle represents one subgroup labeled by its leader's name. The size of the circle is proportional to the number of criminals in the group. A line represents a relationship between two groups. The thickness represents the strength of the relationship.

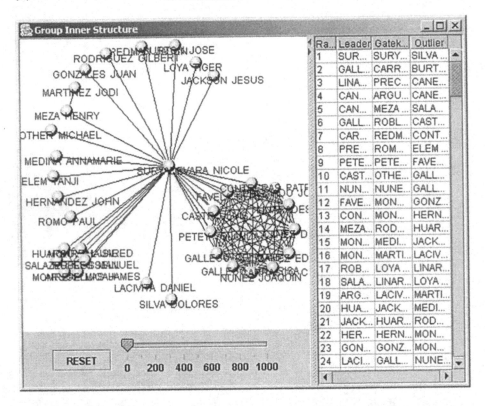

Ra...	Leader	Gatek...	Outlier
1	SUR...	SURY...	SILVA ...
2	GALL...	CARR...	BURT...
3	LINA...	PREC...	CANE...
4	CAN...	ARGU...	CANE...
5	CAN...	MEZA ...	SALA...
6	GALL...	ROBL...	CAST...
7	CAR...	REDM...	CONT...
8	PRE...	ROM...	ELEM ...
9	PETE...	PETE...	FAVE...
10	CAST...	OTHE...	GALL...
11	NUN...	NUNE...	GALL...
12	FAVE...	MON...	GONZ...
13	CON...	MON...	HERN...
14	MEZA...	ROD...	HUAR...
15	MON...	MEDI...	JACK...
16	MON...	MARTI...	LACIV...
17	ROB...	LOYA ...	LINAR...
18	SALA...	LINAR...	LOYA ...
19	ARG...	LACIV...	MARTI...
20	HUA...	JACK...	MEDI...
21	JACK...	HUAR...	ROD...
22	HER...	HERN...	MON...
23	GON...	GONZ...	MON...
24	LACI...	GALL...	NUNE...

Figure 7-2c. The inner structure of the biggest group (the relationships between group members). Centrality rankings of members in this group are listed in a table at the right-hand side.

- *Interaction patterns identified could help reveal relationships that previously had been overlooked.* Our system could generate the "big picture" for a complex network. As a result some relationships between criminal groups that were overlooked before could become easier to identify.

- *Saving investigation time.* Our domain experts obtained knowledge about the gang and narcotics organizations during several years of work. Using information gathered from a large number of arrests and interviews, they built the networks incrementally by linking new criminals to known gangs in the network and then studying the organization of these networks. Because there was no structural analysis tool available, they did all this work by hand. With the help of our system, they expected substantial time could be saved in network creation and structural analysis.

- *Saving training time for new investigators.* New investigators who did not have sufficient knowledge of criminal organizations and individuals could use the system to grasp the essence of the network and crime history quickly. They would not have to spend a significant amount of time studying hundreds of incident reports.

- *Helping prove guilt of criminals in court.* The relationships discovered between individual criminals and criminal groups would be helpful for proving guilt when presented at court for prosecution.

7.3   Case Study 9: Domestic Extremist Groups on the Web

Although not as well-known as some of the international terrorist organizations, the extremist and hate groups within the United States also pose a significant threat to our national security. Recently, these groups have been intensively utilizing the Internet to advance their causes. Thus, to understand how the domestic extremist and hate groups develop their web presence is very important in addressing domestic terrorism threats. This study proposes the development of systematic methodologies to capture domestic extremist and hate groups' web site data and support subsequent analyses. In this study, we aim to answer the following research questions:

- What are the most appropriate techniques for collecting high-quality web pages of domestic extremist and hate groups?

- What are the systematic procedures for analyzing and visualizing the content of these individual web sites?

We propose a sequence of semi-automated methods to study domestic extremist and hate group content on the web. First, we employ a semi-automatic procedure to harvest and construct a high-quality domestic terrorist web site collection. We then perform hyperlink analysis based on a clustering algorithm to reveal the relationships between these groups. Lastly, we conduct an attribute-based content analysis to determine how these groups use the web for their purposes. Because the procedure adopted in this study is similar to that reported in Case Study 3, Jihad on the Web, we only summarize selected interesting results below.

- *Collection Building:* We manually extracted a set of URLs from relevant literature. In particular, the web sites of the "Southern Poverty Law Center" (SPLC, www.splcenter.org) and the Anti-Defamation League (ADL, www.adl.org) are authoritative sources for identifying domestic extremists and hate groups. A total of 266 seed URLs were identified in SPLC and the ADL web sites as well as in the Google directory. A backlink expansion of this initial set was performed and the count increased to 386 URLs. The resulting set of URLs is validated by an expert. A total of 97 URLs were deemed relevant. We then spidered and downloaded all of the web documents within the identified web sites. As a result, our final collection contained about 400,000 documents.

- *Hyperlink Analysis:* Using the MDS algorithm (Torgerson, 1952), we visualize the hidden hyperlinked communities among 35 web sites randomly retrieved from our collection. Several communities are identified in the network shown in Figure 7-3. The top-left side of the network shows the "Neo-Confederate" cluster, which mainly consists of the web sites of new confederate organizations in the Southern states. They espouse a separatist ideology, promoting the establishment of an independent state in the south. In addition, they share elements of white supremacy ideas with other non-neo-confederate racist organizations such as the KKK. A cluster of web sites of white supremacists occupies the top-right corner of the network, including: Stormfront, White Aryan Resistance, etc. Christian Identity, Militia, and Eco-Terrorism clusters were also identified.

- *Content Analysis:* We asked our domain experts to review each web site in our collection and record the presence of low-level attributes based on an eight-attribute coding scheme: Sharing Ideology, Propaganda (Insiders), Recruitment and Training, Command and Control, Virtual Community, Propaganda (Outsiders), Fundraising, and Communications. For instance, the web page of "Nation of Islam" contains recordings of the organization's leaders (for their followers). The presence of these recordings contributes to the web site's content richness and is coded under the "Propaganda (Insiders)" attribute. Our web coding scheme is similar in nature to the one developed by Demchak et al. (2000) for coding government web site characteristics.

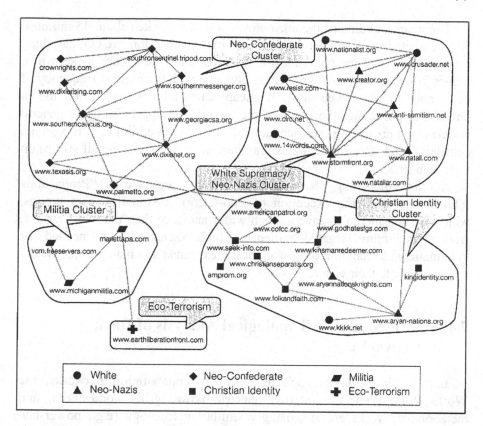

Figure 7-3. Web community visualization of selected domestic extremist and hate groups.

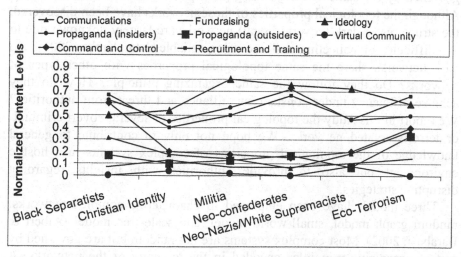

Figure 7-4. Content analysis of selected web sites of domestic extremist and hate groups.

The manual coding of the attributes in a web site takes about 45 minutes. After completing coding for the web sites in our collection, we compared the content of each of the six domestic extremist and hate groups as shown in Figure 7-4. "Sharing Ideology" is the attribute with the highest frequency of occurrence in these web sites. It encapsulates all communication media devoted to portraying the goals of the terrorist group, defining its general policies, and presenting the foundational ideology. In addition, "Propaganda (Insiders)" and "Recruitment and Training" are widely used by all groups on their web sites.

Another interesting observation is the low presence of "Propaganda (Outsiders)," with the exception of Eco-terrorism/Animal Rights groups, which are considered to have a much wider audience than the racist groups, who have a more targeted audience. Much research is still needed for systematic understanding of how domestic extremist and hate groups use the web to promote their causes.

7.4   Case Study 10: Topological Analysis of Dark Networks

Large-scale networks such as scientific collaboration networks, the World Wide Web, the Internet, electric power grids, food webs, and metabolic networks are surprisingly similar in topology (e.g., power-law degree distribution), leading to a conjecture that complex systems are governed by the same self-organizing principle (Albert & Barabasi, 2002). Although the topological properties of these networks have been discovered, the structures of dark (covert, illegal) networks are largely unknown due to the difficulty of collecting and accessing reliable data (Krebs, 2001). Do dark networks share the same topological properties with other types of networks? Do they follow the same organizing principle? How do they achieve efficiency under constant surveillance and threat from authorities? We report in this study the topological properties of several covert criminal- or terrorist-related networks. We hope not only to contribute to general knowledge of the topological properties of complex systems in a hostile environment but also to provide authorities with insights regarding disruptive strategies.

Three models have been employed to characterize complex networks: random graph model, small-world model, and scale-free model (Albert & Barabasi, 2002). Most complex systems are not random but are governed by certain organizing principles encoded in the topology of the networks. A small-world network has a significantly larger clustering coefficient than its random model counterpart while maintaining a relatively small average path length. The large clustering coefficient indicates that there is a high tendency for nodes to form communities and groups. Scale-free networks, on the other hand, are characterized by the power-law degree distribution, meaning that while a large number of nodes in the network have just a few links, a small fraction of the nodes have a large number of links. It is believed that scale-free networks evolve following the self-organizing principle, where growth and preferential attachment play a key role for the emergence of the power-law degree distribution.

We studied the topology of four covert networks: the Global Salafi Jihad (GSJ) terrorist network (Sageman, 2004), a narcotics trafficking criminal network (Xu & Chen, 2003; Xu & Chen, Forthcoming) whose members mainly deal with methamphetamines, a gang criminal network, and a terrorist web site network (Chen *et al.*, 2004). The 366-member GSJ network was constructed based entirely on open source data but all nodes and links were examined and carefully validated by a domain expert. The "Meth World" consists of 1,349 criminals who were involved in methamphetamine-related crimes in Tucson, Arizona, between 1985 and 2002. The gang network consists of 3,917 criminals who were involved in gang-related crimes in Tucson between 1985 and 2002. In the two criminal networks, two members are connected if they committed at least one crime together. Based on reliable governmental sources, we also identified 104 web sites created by four major international terrorist groups. Hyperlinks were used as between-site relations.

Each network contains many small components and a single giant component (see Table 7-1). We focused only on the giant component in these networks and performed topology analysis and robustness analysis. We found that all these networks are small worlds (see Table 7-2). The average path lengths and diameters of these networks are small with respect to their network sizes. Thus, a terrorist or criminal can connect with any other member in a network through just a few mediators. In addition, these networks are quite sparse with very low link density. These two properties have important implications to the efficiency of transmission of goods and information within the networks. Because the risk of being detected by authorities increases as more people are involved, the small path length and link sparseness can help lower risks and enhance efficiency. In addition, we calculated the path length of a node to a central node, a measure which is called "Erdős number" in the network of mathematicians. This measure is also related to the closeness centrality, defined as the total path length from a specific node to all other nodes in a network. We found that members in the criminal and terrorist networks are extremely close to their leaders. The terrorists in the GSJ network are on average only 2.5 steps away from bin Laden, meaning that bin Laden's command can reach an arbitrary member through only two mediators. Similarly, the average path length to the leader in the Meth World is only 3.9. Such a short chain of command means communication efficiency. However, special attention should be paid to the Dark Web. Despite its small size (80), the average path length is 4.70, larger than that (4.20) of the GSJ network, which has almost 9 times more nodes. Since hyperlinks help visitors navigate between web pages, and because terrorist web sites are often used for soliciting new members and donations, the relatively long path length may be due to the reluctance of terrorist groups to share potential resources with other terrorist groups.

The other small-world topology, high clustering coefficient, is also present in these dark networks. The clustering coefficients of these four networks are significantly higher than those of random graph counterparts. Previous studies have also shown the evidence of groups and teams in these networks. In these groups and teams, members tend to have denser and stronger relations with one another. The communication between group members becomes more efficient, making a crime or an attack easier to plan, organize, and execute.

In addition, these dark networks are scale-free systems. The three human networks have an exponentially truncated power-law degree distribution (see Table 7-1 and Figure 7-5). Different from other types of networks whose exponents usually are between 2.0 and 3.0, the exponents of dark networks are fairly small. The degree distribution decays much more slowly for small degrees than for that of other types of networks, indicating a higher frequency for small degrees.

Table 7-1. The statistics and parameters in the exponentially truncated power-law degree distribution of the dark networks.

	GSJ	Meth World	Gang Network	Dark Web
Number of Nodes	366	1349	3917	104
Number of Links	1247	4784	9051	156
Size of Giant Component	356 (97.3%)	924 (68.5%)	2231 (57.0%)	80 (77.9%)
Link Density	0.02	0.01	0.003	0.05
Average Degree, <k>	6.97	4.62	2.87	1.94
Exponent, γ	0.67	1.41	1.11	1.33
Cutoff, κ	15.35	23.60	14.65	34.59

At the same time, the exponential cutoff implies that the distribution for large degrees decays faster than is expected for a power-law distribution, preventing the emergence of large hubs which have many links.

Two possible reasons have been suggested that may attenuate the effect of growth and preferential attachment: (a) the aging effect: as time progresses some older nodes may stop receiving new links, and (b) the cost effect: as maintaining links induces costs (Hummon, 2000), there is a constraint on the maximum number of links a node can have. We believe that the aging effect does exist in the dark networks. In the Meth World, for example, some criminals who were present in the network several years ago may have become inactive due to arrest or death, and thus could not receive new links even though they are still included in the network. Moreover, the cost of links takes the form of risks. Under constant threat from authorities, criminals or terrorists may avoid attaching to too many people, limiting the effects of preferential attachment.

Table 7-2. The small-world properties of the dark networks.

	GSJ		Meth World		Gang Network		Dark Web	
	Real	Random	Real	Random	Real	Random	Real	Random
Average Path Length	4.20	3.23	6.49	4.52	9.56	6.23	4.70	3.35
Diameter	9	6.00	17	9.57	22	16.40	12	13.16
Clustering Coefficient	0.55	0.2×10^{-1}	0.60	0.5×10^{-1}	0.68	0.6×10^{-3}	0.47	0.1×10^{-1}

Evidence has shown that hubs in criminal networks may not be the real leaders. Another possible constraint on preferential attachment is trust (Krebs, 2001). This constraint is especially common in the GSJ network where the terrorists preferred to attach to those who were their relatives, friends, or religious partners.

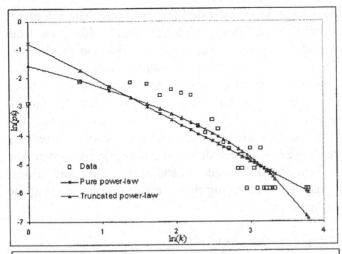

Figure 7-5.
The degree
distributions (x-axis:
ln(k); y-axis: ln(p_k)).
Figure 7-5a.
The degree
distribution of the
GSJ network.

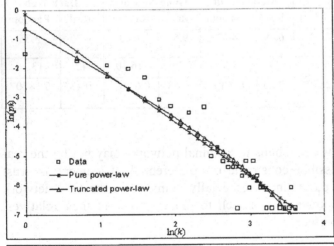

Figure 7-5b.
The degree
distribution of the
Meth World.

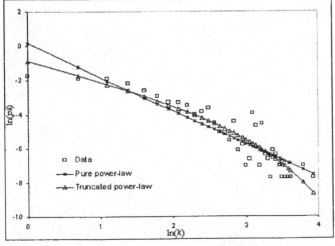

Figure 7-5c.
The degree
distribution of the
gang network.

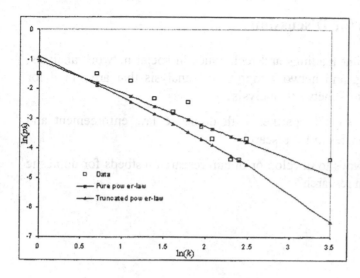

Figure 7-5d.
The degree
distribution of the
Dark Web.

7.5   Future Directions

As terrorists may be involved in local crimes and conduct their acts in local jurisdictions, state and local law enforcement agencies are crucial in fighting terrorism. International terrorists may also leverage the covert gang, narcotic, and people smuggling networks to evade law enforcement investigation and capture. The tragic event of the Oklahoma City bombing shows the continuous threat of domestic extremist and terrorist groups. Information technologies can help find relationships between criminals and (domestic and international) terrorists.

We believe network mining, network visualization, and network topological analysis techniques are invaluable for understanding criminal and terrorist networks. Instead of studying single criminal entities or pairs of entities, we need to study criminals and terrorists using a network perspective. However, we also see a pressing need to develop new theories and principles based on the unique characteristics of the "dark networks" – covertness effect, law enforcement disruption effect, criminal aging effect, religious influence effect, etc. Criminology, criminal psychology, public policy, and terrorism research can potentially contribute to the study of dark networks.

7.6 Questions for Discussion

1. What are important readings and techniques in social network analysis, network learning, and network topological analysis that are suited for criminal and terrorist network analysis?

2. What are some ways to partner with domestic law enforcement and public safety agencies in ISI research?

3. What are some ways to develop or obtain research testbeds for domestic counter-terrorism research?

Chapter 8

PROTECTING CRITICAL INFRASTRUCTURE AND KEY ASSETS

Chapter Overview

The Internet is a critical infrastructure and asset in the information age. However, cyber criminals have been using various web-based channels (e.g., email, web sites, Internet newsgroups, and Internet chat rooms) to distribute illegal materials. One common characteristic of these channels is anonymity. Compared with conventional crimes, cybercrime conducted through such anonymous channels imposes unique challenges for researchers and law enforcement and intelligence agencies in criminal identity tracing. Law enforcement and intelligence agencies have an urgent need for approaches that automate criminal and terrorist identity tracing in cyberspace. Three case studies in this chapter demonstrate the potential of using multilingual authorship analysis with carefully selected writing style feature sets and effective classification techniques for identity tracing in cyberspace.

8.1   Case Study 11: Identity Tracing in Cyberspace

With the rapid proliferation of Internet technologies and applications, cybercrime has become a major concern for the law enforcement community. Cyber criminals have been distributing messages on the Internet to conduct illegal activities. The anonymous nature of online message distribution has made criminal identity tracing a critical problem in cybercrime investigation. We developed a framework for authorship identification of online messages to address the identity tracing problem. In this framework, three types of writing style features are extracted and inductive learning algorithms are used to build feature-based classification models to identify authorship of online messages.

Data used in this study were from open sources. Three datasets, two in English and one in Chinese, were collected. One of the English datasets consisted of 153 USENET newsgroup illegal sales of pirate CDs and software messages. We manually identified the nine most active users (represented by a unique ID and email address) who frequently posted messages in these newsgroups. The Chinese dataset contained 70 Bulletin Board System (BBS) illegal CD and software for-sale messages downloaded from a popular Chinese BBS.

The two key techniques used in this study were feature selection and classification. The objective was to classify text messages into different classes with each class representing one author. Based on the review of previous studies on text and email authorship analysis, along with the specific characteristics of the messages in our datasets, we selected a large number of features that were potentially useful for identifying message authors. Three types of features were used: *style markers* (content-free features such as frequency of function word, total number of punctuations, average sentence length, etc.), *structural features* (such as use of a greeting statement, use of farewell statement, etc.), and *content-specific features* (such as frequency of keywords, special character of content, etc.). Many additional metrics were used in our study as described in Figures 8-1, 8-2, and 8-3.

For classification analysis, three popular classifiers were selected, including the C4.5 decision tree algorithm (Quinlan, 1986), backpropagation neural networks (Lippmann, 1987), and support vector machines (Cristianini & Shawe-Taylor, 2000; Hsu & Lin, 2002). Each individual classifier has been employed in previous authorship analysis research (Diederich et al., 2000). In general SVM and neural networks have better performance than decision trees (Diederich et al., 2000). However, most previous authorship studies were based on newspaper articles such as the *Federalist Papers*. Because online messages are quite different from formal articles in style and length, we needed to test the performances of these algorithms on our datasets.

Additional style markers in this experiment:
    Total number of words in subject
    Total number of characters in subject (S)
    Total number of upper-case characters in words in subject/S
    Total number of punctuations in subject/S
    Total number of white-space characters in subject/S
    Total number of lines
    Total number of characters

   * We used 122 function words and 48 markers suggested by de Vel (de Vel et al., 2001). Another 28 of the most common function words from the *Oxford English Dictionary* and seven other markers were also included.

Figure 8-1. Style markers (205 features).

Additional structural features in this experiment:
    Types of signature (name, title, organization, email, URL, phone number).
    Uses special characters (e.g. ---------) to separate message body and signature.

   * These additional structural features were used with the email dataset only. In the newsgroup messages used in this experiment, no attachment or re-quoted text was allowed.

Figure 8-2. Structural features (9 features).

Has a price in subject
Position of price in message body
Has a contact email address in message body
Has a contact URL in message body
Has a contact phone number
Uses a list of products
Position of product list in body message
Indicates product categories in list
Format of product list

Figure 8-3. Content-specific features (9 features, for newsgroup messages only).

Three experiments were conducted on the newsgroup dataset with one classifier at a time. First, 205 style markers (67 for Chinese BBS dataset) were used; nine structural features were added in the second run; and nine content-specific features were added in the third run. A 30-fold cross-validation testing method was used in all experiments.

We used *accuracy, recall,* and *precision* to evaluate the prediction performance of the three classifiers. Accuracy represents the overall prediction performance of a classifier. For each particular author, we used precision and recall to measure the effectiveness of a classifier. The three measures are defined in equations (1)-(3).

$$\text{Accuracy} = \frac{\text{Number of messages whose author was correctly identified}}{\text{Total number of messages}} \quad (1)$$

$$\text{Recall} = \frac{\text{Number of messages correctly assigned to the author}}{\text{Total number of messages written by the author}} \quad (2)$$

$$\text{Precision} = \frac{\text{Number of messages correctly assigned to the author}}{\text{Total number of messages assigned to the author}} \quad (3)$$

We summarize the results as follows:

- *SVM and neural networks achieved better performance than the C4.5 decision tree algorithm.* For example, using style markers on the email dataset, the C4.5, neural networks, and SVM achieved accuracies of 74.29%, 81.11%, and 82.86% respectively. SVM also achieved consistently higher accuracies, precision, and recall than the neural networks. However, the performance differences between SVM and neural networks were relatively small. Our results were generally consistent with previous studies, in that neural networks and SVM typically had better performance than decision tree algorithms (Diederich et al., 2000).

- *Using style markers and structural features outperformed using style markers only.* We achieved significantly higher accuracies for all three datasets (*p*-values were all below 0.05) by adopting the structural features. This possibly resulted from an author's consistent writing patterns present in the message's structural features.

- *Using style markers, structural features, and content-specific features did not outperform using style markers and structural features.* The results indicated that using content-specific features as additional features did not improve the authorship prediction performance significantly (with p-value of 0.3086). We thought this was because authors of illegal messages typically delivered diverse contents in their messages and little additional information could be derived from the message contents to determine the authorship. We also observed that high accuracies were obtained using only style markers as input features for the English datasets. The accuracies ranged from 71% to 89%. The results indicated that style markers alone contain a large amount of information about people's online message writing styles and were surprisingly robust in predicting the authorship.

- *There is a significant drop in prediction performance measures for the Chinese BBS dataset compared with the English datasets.* For example, when using style markers only, C4.5 achieved average accuracies of 86.28% and 74.29% for the English newsgroup and email datasets, while for the Chinese dataset it only achieved an average accuracy of 54.83%. A possible reason was that only 67 Chinese style markers were used in our current experiments, significantly fewer than the 205 style markers used with the English dataset. We expect to achieve higher prediction performances if additional Chinese style markers are identified and included. We also observed that when structural features were added all three algorithms achieved relatively high precision, recall, and accuracies (from 71% to 83%) for the Chinese dataset. Considering the significant language differences, our proposed approach to the problem of online message identity tracing appears promising in a multilingual context.

8.2   Case Study 12: Feature Selection for Writeprint

Unlike conventional crimes, there are no fingerprints to be found in cybercrime. Fortunately, there is another type of print, which we call "writeprint," hidden in people's writings. Similar to fingerprints, writeprint is composed of multiple features, such as vocabulary richness, length of sentences, use of function words, layout of paragraphs, and keywords. These writeprint features can represent an author's writing style, which is usually consistent across his or her writings, and further become the basis of authorship analysis. This study is aimed at introducing a method of identifying the key writeprint features for authors of online messages to facilitate identity tracing in cybercrime investigation.

A number of studies have shown the discriminating power of different types of features. Furthermore, researchers attempt to identify an optimal set of features for authorship identification. Most previous studies of feature choice compared different types of features. Even if a type of feature is effective for authorship identification, some features in this type may be irrelevant or redundant, hence reducing the prediction accuracy. For instance, de Vel et al. observed a reduction in performance when the number of function word features was increased from 122 to 320 (de Vel, 2001). Feature selection should be undertaken to remove features that do not contribute to prediction. However, few studies have been conducted to select key features for authorship identification at the individual feature level. In addition, extracting a large number of features from online messages is time-consuming and may induce errors. Therefore, it is important to identify the key writeprint features for authorship identification of online messages. Due to the multilingual characteristic of online messages, in this study we examine writeprint features for different languages, i.e., English and Chinese.

Since features are regarded as an abstract representation of writeprint, the quality of the feature selection directly influences this representation. Feature selection techniques aim to select a subset of features that are relevant to the target concept, i.e., writeprint in this study. There are a variety of well developed methods in the pattern recognition and data mining domains to identify important features. Liu and Motoda summarized past studies of feature selection in a general framework (Liu & Motoda, 1998). The process of feature selection can be viewed as a search problem in feature space. Exhaustive search and heuristic search are two major search strategies. In this study we proposed a genetic algorithm-based (GA) feature selection model to identify writeprint features. In such a model each chromosome represents a feature subset, where its length is the total number of candidate features, and each bit indicates whether a feature is selected or not. Thus, the fitness value of each chromosome is defined as the accuracy of the corresponding classifier. By applying genetic operators in the successive generations, the GA model can generate different combinations of features to achieve the highest fitness value. Therefore, the feature subset corresponding to the highest accuracy of classification along all the generations is regarded as the optimum. The selected features in this subset are the key writeprint features to discriminate the writing styles of different authors.

To test the feasibility of authorship identification and to identify the key writeprint features for online messages, the two online message testbeds (English and Chinese) described in the previous section were used. To compare the discriminating power of the full feature set and the optimal set, 30-fold pair-wise t-tests were conducted respectively for the English and Chinese datasets. As shown in Table 8-1, the GA-based model identified a feature subset with about half of the full set as the key features, i.e., 134 out of 270 for English, and 56 out of 114 for Chinese. For the English dataset, the optimal feature set achieved a classification accuracy of 99.01%, which is significantly higher than the 97.85% achieved by the full set (p-value =

0.0417). For the Chinese dataset, the optimal feature set achieved a classification accuracy of 93.56%, which is higher than the 92.42% achieved by the full set, but not significantly (p-value = 0.1270). In general, using the optimal feature subset we can achieve a comparable (if not higher) accuracy of authorship identification.

Table 8-1. Comparison between full feature set and optimal feature subset.

Dataset	Feature set	No. of Features	Mean Accuracy	Variance	P-Value
English	Full set	270	97.85%	0.002	0.0417
	Optimal subset	134	99.01%	0.001	
Chinese	Full set	114	92.42%	0.023	0.1270
	Optimal subset	56	93.56%	0.026	

The effect of feature selection is significant and promising. Furthermore, we discovered that the selected key feature subset included all four types of features. This is consistent with our previous study in (Zheng et al., 2003), which showed that each type of feature contributes to the predictive power of the classification model. In particular, the relatively high proportion of selected structural and content-specific features suggests their useful discriminating power for online messages. Table 8-2 illustrates several key features identified from the full feature set.

Table 8-2. Illustration of key English and Chinese writeprint features.

Feature Type	English	Chinese
Lexical	Total number of upper-case letters /total number of characters; Frequency of character "@" and "$"; Yule's K measure (vocabulary richness); 2-letter word frequency.	Total number of English characters /total number of characters; Total number of digits /total number of characters; Honore's R measure (vocabulary richness).
Syntactic	Frequency of punctuation "!" and ":" Frequency of function word "if" and "can"	Frequency of function word "然后 (then)" and "我想(I think)"
Structural	Number of sentences per paragraph; Has separators	Number of sentences per paragraph; Has separators
Content-specific	Frequency of word "check" and "sale"	Frequency of "音乐(music)" and "小说(novel)"

The results from Table 8-2 have some interesting implications. Since some features in the full feature set may be irrelevant for online messages, the frequency of characters related to online messages (e.g., "@," "$") instead of other common ones (e.g., "A," "E") were selected. In addition, since some features may only provide redundant information, the total number of upper-case letters/ total number of characters was identified as a key feature, while the frequency of lower-case letters was discarded. Similarly, only one vocabulary richness measure, e.g., Yule's K or Honore's R, was selected and others were ignored. Since online messages are often short in length and flexible in style, structural layout traits such as the average length of paragraphs became more useful. In addition, content-specific features are highly related to their context. Hence features such as "sale" and "check" were identified as the key content-specific features for the English dataset based on sales of pirated software/CDs. In other contexts, different content-specific features should be identified and used accordingly. These selected key features of writeprint can effectively represent the distinct writing style of each author and further assist us to identify the authorship of new messages.

8.3   Case Study 13: Developing an Arabic Authorship Model

The evolution of the Internet as a major international communication medium has spawned the advent of a multilingual dimension. Application of authorship identification techniques across multilingual web content is important due to increased globalization and the ensuing security issues that are created.

Arabic is one of the six official languages of the United Nations and the mother tongue of over 300 million people. The language is gaining interest due to its socio-political importance and differences from Indo-European languages. The morphological challenges pertaining to Arabic pose several critical problems for authorship identification techniques. These problems could be partially responsible for the lack of previous authorship analysis studies relating to Arabic.

In this study, we apply an existing framework for authorship identification to Arabic web forum messages. Techniques and features are incorporated to address the specific characteristics of Arabic, resulting in the creation of an Arabic language model. We also present a comparison of English and Arabic language models.

Most previous authorship studies have only focused on English, with a few studies done on Greek and Chinese. Stamamatos et al. applied authorship identification to a corpus of Greek newspaper articles (Stamamtos et al., 2001). Peng et al. conducted experiments on English documents, Chinese novels, and Greek newspapers using an n-gram model

(Peng et al., 2003). Zheng et al. performed authorship identification on English and Chinese web forum messages (Zheng et al., 2003). In all previous studies, English results were better than other languages. Applying authorship identification features across different languages is not without its difficulties. Since most writing style characteristics were designed for English, they may not always be applicable or relevant for other languages. Structural and other linguistic differences can create feature extraction nightmares.

Arabic is a Semitic language, meaning that it belongs to the group of Afro-Asian languages which also includes Hebrew. It is written from right to left with letters in the same word being joined together, similar to English cursive writing. Semitic languages have several characteristics that can cause difficulties for authorship analysis. These challenges include properties such as inflection, diacritics, word length, and elongation.

- Inflection:

Inflection is the derivation of stem words from a root. Although the root has a meaning, it is not a word but rather a class that contains stem instances (words). Stems are created by adding affixes (prefixes, infixes, and suffixes) to the root using specific patterns. Words with common roots are semantically related. Arabic roots are 3-5 letter consonant combinations with the majority being 3-letters. Al-Fedaghi and Al-Anzi believe that as many as 85% of Arabic words are derived from a tri-lateral root, suggesting that Arabic is highly inflectional (Al-Fedaghi and Al-Anzi, 1989). Inflection can cause feature extraction problems for lexical features because high levels of inflection increase the number of possible words, since a word can take on numerous forms.

- Diacritics:

Diacritics are markings above or below letters, used to indicate special phonetic values. An example of diacritics in English would be the little markings found on top of the letter "e" in the word résumé. These markings alter the pronunciation and meaning of the word. Arabic uses diacritics in every word to represent short vowels, consonant lengths, and relationships between words.

- Word Length:

Arabic words tend to be shorter than English words. The shorter length of Arabic words reduces the effectiveness of many lexical features. The short-word count feature, used to track words whose length is 3-letters or smaller, may have little discriminatory potential when applied to Arabic. Additionally, the word-length distribution may also be less effective since Arabic word-length distributions have a smaller range.

- Elongation:

Arabic words are sometimes stretched out or elongated. This is done for purely stylistic reasons using a special Arabic character that resembles a dash ("-"). Elongation is possible because Arabic characters are joined during writing. Table 8-3 shows an example of elongation. The word MZKR ("remind") is elongated with the addition of four dashes between the "M" and the "Z." Although elongation provides an important authorship identification feature, it can also create problems.

Table 8-3. An Arabic elongation example.

Elongated	English	Arabic	Word Length
No	MZKR	مذكر	4
Yes	M----ZKR	مـــذكر	8

Our testbed consisted of English and Arabic datasets. The English dataset was adapted from Zheng et al.'s study and consists of messages from USENET newsgroups (Zheng et al., 2003). The dataset identifies 20 authors engaged in potentially illegal activities relating to computer software and music sales and trading. The data consists of 20 messages per author for a total of 400 messages. The Arabic dataset was extracted from Yahoo groups and is also composed of 20 authors and 20 messages per author. These authors discuss a broader range of topics including political ideologies and social issues in the Arab world. Based on previous studies, there are numerous classification techniques that can provide adequate performance. In this research, we adopted two popular machine learning classifiers; ID3 decision trees and Support Vector Machine (SVM). The Arabic feature set was modeled after the English feature set. It includes 410 features, with the key differences highlighted in Table 8-4.

The results for the comparison of the different feature types and techniques are summarized in Table 8-5 and Figure 8-4. In both datasets the accuracy kept increasing with the addition of more feature types. The maximum accuracy was achieved with the use of SVM and all feature types for English and Arabic. Using all features with the SVM classifier, we were able to achieve an accuracy level of 85.43% for the Arabic dataset; a level lower than the 96.09% achieved for the English dataset.

Table 8-4. Differences between English and Arabic feature sets.

Feature Type	Feature	English	Arabic
Lexical, F1	Short-Word Count	Track all words 3 letters or less	Track all words 2 letters or less
	Word-Length Distribution	1-20 letter words	1-15 letter words
	Elongation	N/A	Track number of elongated words
Syntactic, F2	Function Words	150 words	250 words
	Word Roots	N/A	30 roots
Structural, F3	No Differences	-	-
Content Specific, F4	Number of words	11	25

Table 8-5. Accuracy for different feature sets across techniques.

Accuracy (%)	English Dataset		Arabic Dataset	
Features	C4.5	SVM	C4.5	SVM
F1	86.98%	92.84%	68.07%	74.20%
F1+F2	88.16%	94.00%	73.77%	77.53%
F1+F2+F3	88.29%	94.11%	76.23%	84.87%
F1+F2+F3+F4	89.31%	**96.09%**	81.03%	**85.43%**

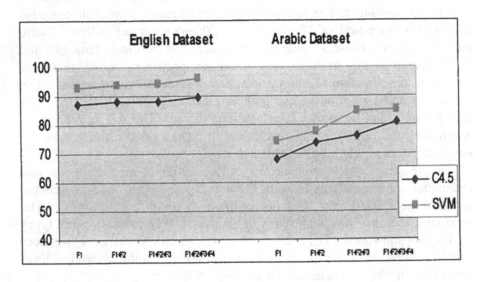

Figure 8-4. Authorship identification accuracies for different feature types and techniques.

A comparison of C4.5 and SVM revealed that SVM significantly outperformed the decision tree classifier in all cases. This is consistent with previous studies that also showed SVM to be superior. The difference between the two classifiers was consistent across English and Arabic, with English accuracies being about 10% higher.

In the future we would like to analyze authorship differences at the group level within a specific language. Identification of unique writing style characteristics for speakers of the same languages across different geographic locations (e.g., Iraq vs. Palestine), cultures (e.g., Sunni vs. Shiite), and interest (e.g., terrorist) groups could prove to be an interesting endeavor.

8.4   Future Directions

Cyber-infrastructure protection and cyber-trust are some of the most pressing ISI research topics of relevance to IT researchers. Unlike traditional critical infrastructure (e.g., highways, bridges, dams, and etc.), cyber-infrastructure can be attacked from any part of the world. The openness of the Internet protocol also invites unwanted and unforeseeable intrusions and disruptions. International terrorists and criminals have long been using the Internet for their illegal and covert activities. Much ISI research is needed in intrusion detection, computer forensics, Internet identity frauds, and grid computing and sensors in the next decade.

8.5   Questions for Discussion

1. What are the research opportunities in NSF cyber-infrastructure and cyber-trust programs? What are some ways to leverage national security research opportunities in these areas?

2. How can grid computing and sensors be incorporated into ISI research?

3. How can multilingual research be applied in cyber-infrastructure protection?

4. What is computer forensics? How can it be applied to the Internet and cyberspace? What are the research opportunities?

Chapter 9
DEFENDING AGAINST CATASTROPHIC TERRORISM

Chapter Overview

Terrorist attacks can cause devastating damage to a society through the use of chemical, biological, or radiological weapons. Biological attacks may cause contamination, infectious disease outbreaks, and significant loss of life. Information systems that can efficiently and effectively collect, access, analyze, and report infectious disease data can help prevent, detect, respond to, and manage these attacks. In this chapter we discuss our ongoing BioPortal research and system development efforts motivated to address some of these challenges.

9.1 Case Study 14: BioPortal for Disease and Bioagent Surveillance

Our initial BioPortal research focuses on two prominent infectious diseases: *West Nile Virus* (WNV) and *Botulism (BOT)*. These two diseases were chosen because of their significant public health and national security implications and the availability of related datasets with our research partners. We developed a research prototype, called the *WNV-BOT Portal* system, which provides integrated, web-enabled access to a variety of distributed data sources including the New York State Department of Health (NYSDOH), the California Department of Health Services (CADHS), and some other federal sources (e.g., United States Geological Survey, USGS). It also provides advanced information visualization capabilities as well as predictive modeling support.

Architecturally, the WNV-BOT Portal consists of three major components: a *web portal*, a *data store*, and a *communications backbone*. The web portal component implements the user interface and provides the following main functionalities: (1) searching and querying available WNV/BOT datasets, (2) visualizing WNV/BOT datasets using spatial-temporal visualization, (3) accessing analysis and prediction functions, and (4) accessing the alerting mechanism.

To enable data interoperability, we use Health Level Seven (HL7) standards (http://www.hl7.org/) as the main storage format. In our data warehousing approach, contributing data providers transmit data to WNV-BOT Portal as HL7-compliant XML messages (through a secure network connection if necessary). To alleviate potential computational performance problems associated with this HL7 XML-based approach, we have identified a core set of data fields based on which searches could be performed efficiently.

An important function of the data store layer is data ingest and access control. The data ingest control module is responsible for checking the integrity and authenticity of data feeds from the underlying information sources. The access control module is responsible for granting and restricting user access to sensitive data.

The communication backbone component enables data exchanges between the WNV-BOT Portal and the underlying WNV/BOT sources based upon the CDC's National Electronic Disease Surveillance System (NEDSS) and HL7 standards. It uses a collection of source-specific "connectors" to communicate with underlying sources. We use the connector linking NYSDOH's Health Information Network (HIN) system and WNV-BOT Portal to illustrate a typical design of such connectors. The data from HIN to the portal system is transmitted in a "push" manner. HIN sends secure Public

Health Information Network Messaging System (PHIN MS) messages to the portal at pre-specified time intervals. The connector at the portal side runs a data receiver daemon listening for incoming messages. After a message is received, the connector checks for data integrity syntactically and invokes the data normalization subroutine. Then the connector stores the verified message in the portal's internal data store through its data ingest control module. Other data sources (e.g., those from USGS) may have "pull"-type connectors which periodically download information from the source web sites and examine and store data in the portal's internal data store.

The WNV-BOT Portal makes available the Spatial Temporal Visualizer (STV) (Buetow et al., 2003) to facilitate exploration of infectious disease case data and to summarize query results. The STV has three integrated and synchronized views: periodic, timeline, and GIS. Figure 9-1 illustrates how these three views can be used to explore an infectious disease dataset. The top-left panel shows the GIS view. The user can select multiple datasets to be shown on the map in a layered manner using the checkboxes. The top-right panel corresponds to the timeline view displaying the occurrences of various cases using a Gantt chart-like display. The user can also access case details easily using the tree display located left of the timeline display. Below the timeline view is the periodic view through which the user can identify periodic temporal patterns (e.g., which months have an unusually high number of cases). The bottom portion of the interface allows the user to specify subsets of data to be displayed and analyzed.

Our project has supported exploration of, and experimentation with, technological infrastructures needed for the full-fledged implementation of a national infectious disease information infrastructure and has helped foster information sharing and collaboration among related government agencies at state and federal levels. In addition, we have obtained important insights and hands-on experience with various important policy-related challenges faced by developing a national infrastructure. For example, a significant part of our project activity has been centered on developing privacy-sensitive data sharing agreements between project partners from different states.

Our ongoing technical research is focusing on two aspects of infectious disease informatics: hotspot analysis and efficient alerting and dissemination. For WNV, localized clusters of dead birds typically identify high-risk disease areas. Automatic detection of dead bird clusters using hotspot analysis can help predict disease outbreaks and allocate prevention/control resources effectively. Initial experimental results indicate that these techniques are promising for disease informatics analysis. We are planning to augment existing predictive models by considering additional environmental factors (e.g., weather information, bird migration patterns) and tailoring data mining techniques for infectious disease datasets that have prominent temporal features.

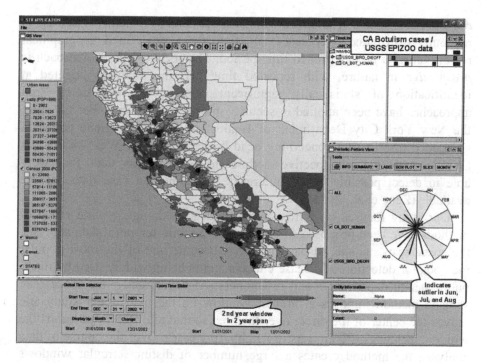

Figure 9-1. Using STV to visualize botulism data.

9.2 Case Study 15: Hotspot Analysis and Surveillance

In infectious disease informatics and bioterrorism studies, measurements of interest are often made at various locations and with timestamps. In the public health domain, the disease cases reported to the Centers for Disease Control and Prevention (CDC) through its National Notifiable Diseases Surveillance System are collected with timestamps at various places across the entire nation. Similar disease case reporting practices exist at state and local jurisdictions, typically with cases identified with specific geo-locations.

Recent years have seen increasing interest in answering the following central questions of great practical importance arising in spatio-temporal data analysis and related predictive modeling: (a) How can we identify areas having exceptionally high or low measures? (b) How can we determine whether the unusual measures can be attributed to known random variations or are statistically significant? In the latter case, how do we assess the explanatory factors? (c) How can we identify any statistically significant changes (e.g., in rates of health syndromes or crime occurrences) in a timely manner in a geographic area?

Two types of approaches have been developed in the literature to address some of these questions. The first type of approach is considered the *retrospective* model. It is aimed at testing statistically whether a disease is randomly distributed over space and time for a predefined geographical region during a predetermined time period. The second type of approach is *prospective* in nature, with repeated time periodic analyses targeted at identification of statistically significant changes in real time. Both approaches have been applied in security informatics practice. For instance, the New York City Department of Health and Mental Hygiene collected geo-coded information concerning dead birds infected by West Nile Virus (WNV). Applying retrospective methods to avian fatality data, they were able to detect possible WNV outbreaks before human case data became available (Zeng et al., 2004).

Our study focuses on retrospective models. Although a wide range of methods have been proposed for retrospective spatio-temporal data analysis, the space scan statistic, in particular, has become one of the most popular methods for detection of disease clusters and is being widely used by many public health departments and researchers. Algorithmically, the space scan statistic method imposes a circular window on the map under study and moves the center of the circle over the area so that at different positions the window includes different sets of neighboring cases. Over the course of data analysis, the method creates a large number of distinct circular windows (other shapes such as rectangle and ellipse have also been used), each with a different set of neighboring areas within it and each a possible candidate for containing a cluster of events. Conditioning on the observed total number of cases, the spatial scan statistic is defined as the maximum likelihood ratio over all possible circles. The likelihood ratio for a circle indicates how likely the observed data are given a differential rate of events within and outside the zone.

Despite its success, there are a number of limitations associated with the scan statistic approach. First, its efficiency depends on the use of simple, fixed symmetrical shapes of regions. As a result, when the real underlying clusters do not conform to such shapes, the identified regions are often not well localized. Second, it is difficult to customize and fine-tune the clustering results using the scan statistic approach. Users often have different needs as to the level of granularity and number of the resulting clusters and they may have different degrees of tolerance regarding outliers.

These limitations have motivated our research aimed at exploring and developing alternative and complementary modeling approaches for spatio-temporal data analysis in the context of security informatics. This case study reports our effort in studying two such approaches: *Risk-adjusted Nearest Neighbor Hierarchical Clustering* (RNNH), which was initially developed for crime analysis; and *Risk-adjusted Support Vector Clustering* (RSVC), a new hotspot analysis approach we have recently developed.

Developed for crime hotspot analysis, RNNH is based on the well-known nearest neighbor hierarchical clustering (NNH) method, combining the hierarchical clustering capabilities with kernel density interpolation techniques. The standard NNH approach identifies clusters of data points that are close together (based on a threshold distance). Many such clusters, however, are due to some background or baseline factors (e.g., the population which is not evenly distributed over the entire area of interest). RNNH is primarily motivated to identify clusters of data points *relative* to the baseline factor. Algorithmically, it dynamically adjusts the threshold distance inversely proportional to some density measure of the baseline factor (e.g., the threshold should be shorter in regions where the population is high). Such density measures are computed using kernel density based on the distances between the location under study and some or all other data points.

RSVC is the result of our recent attempt to combine the risk adjustment idea of RNNH with a modern, robust clustering mechanism such as Support Vector Machines (SVM) to improve the quality of hotspot analysis. SVMs are the most well-known of a class of algorithms that use the idea of kernel substitution. SVM-based data description and novelty detection (DDND) is particularly relevant to our research. SVM-based DDND methods are aimed at identifying the *support* of a data distribution. They can single out data clusters in complex shapes and have been well-tested in complex, noisy domains (e.g., handwritten symbol recognition). The standard version of SVM-based DDND does not take into consideration baseline data points and therefore cannot be directly used in spatio-temporal data analysis. As such, we have developed a *risk-adjusted* variation, called RSVC, based on ideas similar to those in RNNH. In this new approach we first compute the kernel density estimations using the baseline data points and then adjust width parameter in the Gaussian kernel function based on such density estimations.

We have conducted a series of computational studies to evaluate the effectiveness of the three hotspot analysis techniques (Satscan, RNNH, RSVC) discussed above. In our experiment, we used artificially generated datasets with known underlying probability distributions to precisely and quantitatively evaluate the efficacy of these techniques. We use the well-known measures from information retrieval to evaluate the performance of hotspot techniques: Precision, Recall, and F-Measure. In the spatial data analysis context, we define these measures as follows.

Let A denote the size of the hotspot(s) identified by a given algorithm, B the size of the true hotspot(s), and C the size of the overlapped area between the algorithm-identified hotspot(s) and true hotspot(s). Precision is defined as C/A. Recall is defined as C/B. F-measure is defined as the harmonic mean of precision and recall (2 * Precision * Recall / (Precision + Recall)). High recall indicates low false negatives and high precision indicates low false positives. Notice that achieving a high level of one measure often impacts negatively achieving a high level of the other measure.   F-measure represents a balance and trade-off between precision and recall.

We report three artificially-generated scenarios with which we have experimented. In the first scenario, as shown in Figure 9-2, we first randomly generated 100 baseline points in one circle (whose center is around (6.7, 8.2) on the graph).

We then generated 200 case points of interest in total. The first 100 points were generated inside of the baseline circle. (As such, these data points do not represent a new unusual hotspot.) The next 100 points were generated within another circle (whose center is around (14.3, 10.2)). It is clear that the only true hotspot is this second circle.

To make the problem more interesting, we introduced some noise -- 30 outlier baseline points and 40 outlier case points over the entire map. For statistical testing purposes, we repeated the above data generation process 30 times to produce 30 instances of the template scenario by moving the centers of the two circles randomly across the map and also by varying the distances between them so long as they did not overlap.

To collect the performance data, we ran all hotspot analysis methods under study on all the problem instances. Table 9-1 summarizes these methods' average performance across all instances. Overall RSVC achieves the best F-score at 84.5%.

Table 9-1. Average performance of RSVC, SCAN, and RNNH on 30 instances of Scenario 1.

Technique	Precision	Recall	F-measure
RSVC	79.5%	92.4%	**84.5%**
SCAN	54.3%	**92.9%**	65.4%
RNNH	**95.3%**	49.0%	64.0%

Table 9-2. Average performance of RSVC, SCAN, and RNNH on 30 instances of Scenario 2.

Technique	Precision	Recall	F-measure
RSVC	78.5%	72.6%	**75.0%**
SCAN	60.0%	**77.4%**	67.4%
RNNH	**87.9%**	42.3%	56.2%

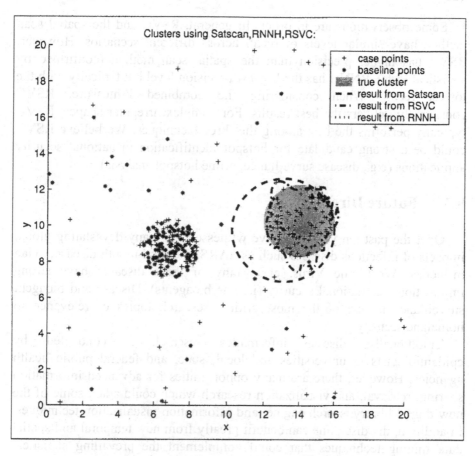

Figure 9-2. Scenario 1 based on simulated data.

Two additional scenarios have been investigated in our study. In Scenario 2, the true hotspots are the two pieces left of a rectangle when its middle section is removed by a circle. In Scenario 3, the true spot is a square with its circular-shaped center removed. The purpose behind the use of these scenarios is to test how robust these hotspot methods are when dealing with hotspots of irregular shape. Tables 9-2 and 9-3 summarize the average performance of these methods when applied to identify hotspots in 30 randomly-generated instances of Scenario 2 and Scenario 3, respectively.

Table 9-3. Average performance of RSVC, SCAN, and RNNH on 30 instances of Scenario 3.

Technique	Precision	Recall	F-Measure
RSVC	84.3%	71.6%	77.2%
SCAN	78.7%	65.0%	69.9%
RNNH	77.0%	24.6%	36.6%

Some observations are in order. In general, RSVC and the spatial scan method have similar levels of recall across different scenarios. However, RSVC has higher precision than the spatial scan method (confirmed by statistical tests). RNNH has the highest precision level but typically with the lowest recall. When considering the combined F-measure, RSVC consistently delivers the best results. For complex, irregular shapes, RSVC typically performs the best among the three techniques. We believe RSVC could be a strong candidate for hotspot identification in national security applications (e.g., disease surveillance, crime hotspot analysis).

9.3   Future Directions

Over the past ten years we have witnessed the many devastating global impacts of infectious diseases such as SARS, foot-and-mouth disease, avian influenza, West Nile Virus, etc. Many of these diseases have strong implications for national security (i.e., as bioagents). Disease and bioagent surveillance is one of the most critical research topics of relevance to homeland security.

Traditionally, disease informatics research is conducted by epidemiologists in universities and local, state, and federal public health agencies. However, there are many opportunities for advanced information sharing, retrieval, and visualization research which could adapt some of the new digital library, search engine, and information visualization techniques. In addition, the discipline can benefit greatly from new temporal and spatial data mining techniques that could complement the prevailing statistical analysis techniques in epidemiology. Standards and ontologies are also critically needed in disease informatics research.

9.4   Questions for Discussion

1. What are the prevailing techniques for disease and syndromic surveillance in epidemiology? What are the assumptions?

2. What is the current status of the BioWatch program at DHS and the BioSense program at CDC? What are their strengths and deficiencies? What are some research opportunities?

3. What are some ways to work with local and state public health agencies on diseases informatics research? What are the available datasets?

4. How should the data confidentiality issue of animal and human disease information be addressed?

5. How can social network analysis and hotspot analysis techniques be applied to other types of diseases? How can other predictive and environmental modeling techniques be incorporated?

Chapter 10

EMERGENCY PREPAREDNESS AND RESPONSE

Chapter Overview

In case of a national emergency, prompt and effective responses are critical to reduce the damage resulting from an attack. In addition to the systems that are designed to defend against catastrophes, information technologies that help develop response plans, identify experts, train response professionals, and manage consequences are beneficial to society. Moreover, information systems that provide social and psychological support to the victims of terrorist attacks can also help society recover from disasters. In this chapter we present two case studies. The first case study uses bibliometric analysis to help identify modern terrorism research experts in the U.S. and internationally. The second case study uses the chatterbot dialog system to help locate terrorism-related information.

10.1   Case Study 16: Mapping Terrorism Research

The recent escalation of global terrorism has attracted a growing number of new, non-traditional research communities owing to the multi-disciplinary dimensions required to gain a better understanding of the terrorism phenomenon. As a result, new researchers face information overload, access, and knowledge discovery challenges. This study provides a longitudinal analysis of terrorism publications from 1965 to 2003, to identify the intellectual structure, changes, and characteristics of the terrorism field. It uses bibliometric and citation analysis to identify core terrorism researchers, their productivity, and knowledge dissemination patterns.

For bibliometric analysis, our initial unit of analysis is the author, whose individual publications, subject areas, journal titles, and institutions provide subsequent analyses. Our first step is to identify a core set of authors and their related publications. We compiled a list of authors from several sources: terrorism publications (Schmid and Jongman, 1988; Reid, 1997), active terrorism experts identified by the KnowNet virtual community (organized by the Sandia National Laboratory), and terrorism research center portals identified on the Internet. Authors identified on the web may represent individuals whose prominence has recently been established or those who have reputable international or non-traditional perspectives on terrorism.

Kennedy and Lum's (2003) list of terrorism research organizations was used to identify a good number of terrorism web-based research portals. We also focused on the Terrorism Research Center (TRC) portal because it is highly recommended by terrorism experts. Using backlink searches in Google, we found thousands of web pages hyperlinked to TRC. We followed TRC's external links to 28 terrorism research organizations and gathered names of terrorism researchers mentioned on the web sites. A total of 131 unique names were identified from using the combined pool of 28 terrorism research center portals, the KnowNet virtual community's recommendations, and those reported by Schmid and Jongman (1988) and Reid (1997).

A bibliography of English-language terrorism publications was compiled for each researcher using commercial databases. The publications include journal articles, books, book chapters, reviews, notes, newspaper articles, conferences papers, and reports. For each core researcher, bibliographic data describing their terrorism-related publications was retrieved. After the citation analysis was conducted, 42 authors were identified as core terrorism researchers based on citation count. A total of 284 researchers/coauthors and their 882 publications made up the sample for this study.

The 42 core researchers are mainly affiliated with academic institutions (23), think tanks (15), media organizations (3), and the government (1). Their bases of operation are located in ten countries including the U.S. (29), the U.K. (4), Ireland (1), Germany (1), Australia (1), Israel (1), Canada (1), France (1), Netherlands (1), and Singapore (1). Specifically, six researchers are from the Rand Corporation including Jenkins, the founder of the Rand terrorism program; three are from the Centre for the Study of Terrorism and Political Violence (CSTPV) at St. Andrews, Scotland; and another three are from the Center for Strategic and International Studies (CSIS), Georgetown University.

To further explore the core terrorism researchers' knowledge creation patterns, authorship data which identify their collaboration patterns and research groups were exploited. There was a high level of coauthorship among the 42 core terrorism researchers where the majority of the researchers (90%) had coauthors. For example, Alexander has 82 coauthors, followed by researchers from the Rand Corporation, such as Jenkins, with 68, Hoffman with 50, and Ronfeldt with 41 coauthors. Wilkinson and Laqueur had less than nine coauthors. They are among the group of core researchers with high author productivity levels. Eight core researchers did not have any coauthors. We also found that Alexander's extensive list of publications is due to his collaborative efforts with 82 coauthors which enabled him to publish books that include 57 anthologies and 10 bibliographies.

Further investigation of the coauthorship relationships provides an understanding of the researchers' collaboration patterns. Figure 10-1 shows the coauthorship network of core terrorism researchers. The nodes represent researchers who coauthored papers.

Some of the most active clusters in the bottom-right corner of Figure 10-1 are the Rand research teams led by Jenkins and Hoffman. Gunaratna, although not employed by Rand, is listed in this cluster because he coauthored publications with Chalk and Hoffman. Hoffman, Gunaratna's Ph.D. advisor at St. Andrews University, Scotland, founded St. Andrews' Centre for the Study of Terrorism and Political Violence (CSTPV) and created the Rand-St. Andrews Terrorism Incident Database, which provides data for their studies (Hughes, 2003).

For the cluster involving Ranstorp (the bottom-left corner of Figure 10-1) from CSTPV, the network is sparse and shares few coauthorships. As chairman of the Advisory Board for CSTPV, Wilkinson has a few collaborations with Alexander but none with researchers at CSTPV who are in this sample. Another cluster includes researchers such as Alexander and Cline (middle of Figure 10-1) at the Center for Strategic and International Studies (CSIS). This cluster displays a pattern of one to many coauthors because Alexander has 82 coauthors. In this particular case, we found that coauthorships do not seem to be sustainable because many authors produced only a single publication with Alexander and did not publish with other terrorism researchers in this sample.

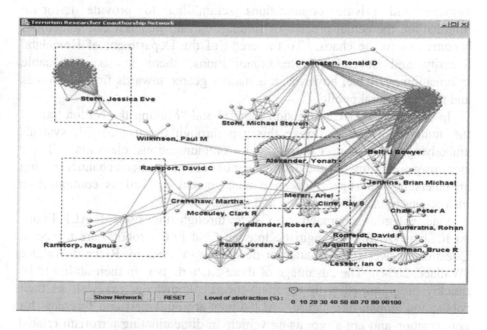

Figure 10-1. Terrorism researchers' coauthorship network.

Since this study is limited to English language publications, 43 of the 131 recommended terrorism researchers have been excluded from our data because their publications were not retrieved. Another inherent limitation of this study brought about by the use of the ISI Web of Science is the exclusion of terrorism studies found in e-journals, congressional testimonials, and recent conference papers as well as non-refereed web materials. This last limitation may have precluded the publications from international, emerging thought leaders.

Despite the foregoing limitations, this study can be seen as significant in that it has assembled useful information that can help lead novice researchers to core terrorism researchers and their key contributions in a challenging field that is growing rapidly. Specifically, it helps identify the most frequently cited terrorism researchers and their publications, dissemination, and collaboration patterns. From this, one may better understand the structure of terrorism research and locate literature produced in particular areas of terrorism. It is a field whose profound implications to our future societies are beyond comprehension.

10.2   Case Study 17: A Dialog System for Terrorism Resources

Terrorism education has become a topic of interest lately. With many agencies and private organizations scrambling to provide terrorism information, the actual process of finding relevant material can sometimes become lost in the chaos. To the credit of the Department of Homeland Security and several private organizations, there is some valuable information available; however, it is mainly geared towards first responders and not the general public.

In both the "9-11 Commission Report" and "Making the Nation Safer," the authors propose to bridge this gap through the use of C3; systems embodying Command, Control, and Communications elements. These systems would allow for the deployment of communications channels during an emergency to support decision management as well as communicate instructions to the public (Moore and Gibbs, 2003).

One potential approach to C3 is through the use of ALICEbots. ALICEbots (Artificial Linguistic Internet Chat Entity robots) are a type of Question-Answer (QA) chatterbot developed in 1995 by Richard Wallace (Wallace, 2004). The advantage of these chatterbots is in their ability to be quickly programmed with terrorism-specific knowledge, as well as their robust and human-like nature. ALICEbots are built first and foremost for conversation and are a promising vehicle in disseminating terrorism-related information to the public.

ALICEbots work by matching user input against pre-existing XML-based input patterns and returning the template response. This simple method of conversational mimicking eliminates the computational overhead that would normally be associated with deeper reasoning systems. The technique can also permit expansion into new knowledge domains, allowing the ALICEbot to convey an 'expert appearance' (Wallace, 2004).

In our research, we aimed to examine the efficacy of shallow Question-Answer (QA) systems for disseminating terrorism-related information to the general public. We created three modified ALICEbots, which differed from each other on the dimension of terrorism knowledge bases used. One chatterbot used only general conversational knowledge, the second used only terrorism domain knowledge, and the third was a combination of both conversation and terrorism knowledge. Referred to as TARA (Terrorism Activity Resource Application) in our research, our system design was based on a modified version of the ALICE Program D chatterbot engine which is freely available at www.ALICEbot.org. There are some notable differences between TARA and ALICE, as illustrated in Table 10-1. The only component that remained unaltered was the actual Chat Engine.

Table 10-1. Differences between Original ALICE Program D and the TARA chatterbot.

	Chat UI	Chat Engine	AIML	Logging	Evaluation
Original ALICE	Uses XML to chat with users	Uses off the shelf ALICE Program D	Uses the freely available Standard and Wallace set (Dialog)	Logs everything to a monolithic XML Log file	None
TARA	Uses a customized perl skin to chat and for evaluation purposes	Same as Original ALICE	Depends on the bot as to whether it is Dialog or customized Terrorism knowledge	Keeps XML logs on a per user basis	Customized perl script that allows users to evaluate and suggest new patterns

We used three chatterbots with differing knowledge bases. The control chatterbot "Dialog," the general conversationalist, was loaded with the standard knowledge set that allowed ALICE to win the early Loebner contests (of machine conversation). This set consists of 41,873 knowledge-based entries. The second chatterbot "Domain," was loaded with 10,491 terrorism-related entries. The third chatterbot "Both," was a summation of "Dialog" and "Domain," which can carry on a general conversation and easily handle terrorism inquiries as well. It contains 52,354 entries, 10 less than a true summation because of an overlap between the dialog and domain knowledge bases.

Terrorism entries were collected through a mixture of automatic and manual means. The majority were gathered automatically from several reputable web sites including http://www.terrorismanswers.com and http://www.11-sept.org. Manual entry was used sparingly to augment the terrorism knowledge set.

For our system comparison research we used ninety participants, thirty for each chatterbot, who were a mixture of undergraduate and graduate students taking various Management of Information Systems classes. Participants were randomly assigned to one of the chatterbots, asked to interact with the system for approximately one-half hour, and permitted to talk about any terrorism-related topic.

The evaluation method of chatterbot responses was an integrated process where users would chat a line and then immediately evaluate the chatterbot's response. Users were asked to evaluate each line with the following two measures; appropriateness of response (Yes/No), and satisfaction level of the response using a Likert scale of values (1-7). Users were also given the opportunity to provide open-ended comments on a line by line basis.

Measurements were conducted on the appropriateness and satisfaction rating of the chatterbot responses. Because the "Both" chatterbot is composed of dialog and domain parts, we took the "Both" chatterbot and broke its responses into its constituent parts of dialog and domain. We then compared those results against the actual Dialog and Domain chatterbots. This comparison is shown in Table 10-2.

Table 10-2. Comparing the components of "Both" against the Dialog and Domain chatterbots.

Comparison	Both's components		Actual chatterbots	
Breakdown of numbers	Dialog	Domain	Dialog	Domain
Number of lines entered into the chatterbot	888	250	1,524	849
Average response appropriateness	68.4%	39.6%	66.3%	21.6%
Average response satisfaction rating	4.51	3.14	4.04	2.43
Standard deviation of response satisfaction	2.12	2.17	2.00	1.90

When comparing the dialog component of "Both" against the actual Dialog chatterbot, the "Both" component rated higher in response appropriateness, 68.4% to 66.3%, as per our expectation. When looking at the domain component of "Both" against the Domain chatterbot, again the "Both" component rated higher, 39.6% compared to 21.6%. Likewise, Response Satisfaction scores from the "Both" chatterbot rate higher than the corresponding "Actual" chatterbots. This analysis shows that the "Both" chatterbot performed better in its constituent areas compared against the stand-alone chatterbots. We believe that this is the result of the dialog portion responding to unrecognized queries and steering communication back to terrorism topics.

We investigated the input/response pairs of the "Both" chatterbot. In particular we were interested in only those user inputs which were in the form of a question (68.4% of the terrorism domain inputs were interrogatives). Table 10-3 summarizes the most frequently observed interrogatives.

Table 10-3. Most frequently observed interrogatives.

Interrogative	Percentage Use
What	27.5%
Do	15.8%
Who	11.1%
How	8.2%
Where	5.8%
Is	5.3%

Investigating the interrogatives further, it was found that the interrogative "what" started the most user queries at 27.5% of all queries. We had expected that interrogatives beginning with "wh*" would be the most prevalent and indeed they were, making up 51.5% of all interrogatives. It is interesting to note how often "Do" and "Is" were used, as these were unexpected surprises. In the vein of work done by Moore and Gibbs (2003) where students used the chatterbot as a search engine, focusing future efforts of knowledge collection at these selected interrogatives should best improve chatterbot accuracy.

In the future, it would be a good idea to investigate adding more knowledge to the system. Although our domain-specific knowledge base appeared to be sufficient for the task, it would be interesting to test even larger corpuses of knowledge and see what impact they may have over dialog knowledge. Another possible aspect worth considering is the addition of a C3 variant, the "I'm Alive" boards. Following the September 11th attacks, multiple boards sprang up around New York City announcing the names and present shelter location of survivors to concerned friends and family members outside of the disaster area. Adding such functionality would be a simple programming exercise and would provide a quicker and more concerted way for bidirectional communications.

10.3 Future Directions

There is little academic research in addressing the needs of the first responders and general public during and after a tragic terrorist event. The devastating effects of such an event often cause significant communication, psychological, and societal chaos well beyond the physical and monetary damages the attack has created. Under the support of the NSF Digital Government Program, several workshops have been conducted to address the needs of the emergency response community. Both technical (e.g., communication interoperability, rescue robots, and disaster relief logistics) and policy (e.g., emergency response authority and plan) challenges and research opportunities were identified. The workshops suggested new funding in emergency preparedness and response research and proposed an academic-agency partnership in addressing short-term and long-term research issues.

10.4   Questions for Discussion

1. Who are the first responders and what are some ways to initiate a research partnership with them?

2. What are the immediate needs of the emergency response and disaster relief community? How can information technologies help with their activities?

3. What are some ways to prepare and educate the general public about terrorism and terrorist events? How can information technologies help with such activities?

4. What are some ways to solicit the help of terrorism researchers to address the various social dimensions and consequences of terrorist events?

5. How can the media help in uncovering the myths of terrorism and educating the public? How can the Internet help in such activities?

Chapter 11

THE PARTNERSHIP AND COLLABORATION FRAMEWORK

Chapter Overview

ISI research requires a close partnership between academic researchers and agency practitioners. Researchers would benefit from the testbed and inputs provided by domain experts. On the other hand, law enforcement and intelligence practitioners could leverage advanced information technologies for their works. However, developing a win-win relationship is not always easy. Agencies often have a pressing and immediate need that cannot wait for long-term, academic research. Data confidentiality concerns may often create barriers for collaboration. In this chapter we present selected research collaboration challenges facing ISI researchers and describe our COPLINK project experience in addressing these challenges. In particular, we present samples of a user data license and Memorandum of Understanding (MOU) that are useful for national security research and collaboration partnership.

11.1 Introduction

To accomplish the six critical mission areas of national security the Department of Homeland Security has proposed to establish a network of laboratories consisting of satellite research centers of excellence across the nation. The purpose is to create a multidisciplinary environment for developing technologies to counter various threats to homeland security. However, information sharing and collaboration across different jurisdictions, agencies, and research institutes is not merely a technical issue. A variety of social, organizational, and political barriers need to addressed, including:

- *Security and confidentiality.* In the intelligence and law enforcement domain, security is of great concern. Data regarding crimes, criminals, terrorist organizations, and potential terrorist attacks may be highly sensitive and confidential. Improper use of data could lead to fatal consequences.

- *Trust and willingness to share information.* Different agencies may not be motivated to share information and collaborate if there is no immediate gain. They may also fear that information being shared would be misused, resulting in legal liabilities.

- *Data ownership and access control.* Who owns a particular dataset? Who is allowed to access, aggregate, or input data? Who owns the derivative data (knowledge)? For both original and derivative data, who is allowed to distribute them to whom?

As a leading research center for law enforcement and intelligence information and knowledge management, the NSF COPLINK Center at the Artificial Intelligence (AI) Lab of the University of Arizona is intended to become a part of the national network of ISI research laboratories. During its development over the past decade the COPLINK Center has encountered many of these non-technical challenges in its partnerships with various law enforcement and federal agencies. We present some of our experiences and lessons learned in this section.

11.2 Ensuring Data Security and Confidentiality

In any information sharing initiative, it is essential to make sure that the data shared between agencies is secure and that the privacy of individuals is respected. In our research we have taken the necessary measures to ensure data privacy, security, and confidentiality. Data shared between law enforcement agencies, such as the Tucson Police Department (TPD),

Phoenix Police Department (PPD), and Tucson Customs and Border Patrol (CBP), contained only law enforcement data and was available only to individuals screened by these agencies using a combination of TPD Background Check, Employee Non-Disclosure Agreement (NDA), and the Terminal Operator Certificate (TOC) test.

All personnel who have access to law enforcement data fill out background forms provided by TPD and have their fingerprints taken at TPD. They also sign a non-disclosure agreement provided by TPD. In addition, they take the TOC test every year. The background information and fingerprints are then checked by TPD investigators to ensure lack of involvement in criminal activity and for verification of identity.

In addition to the above forms and test, all law enforcement data in the University of Arizona's COPLINK Center reside behind a firewall and in a secure room accessible only by activated cards to those who have met the above security criteria. As soon as an employee stops working on projects related to law enforcement data, their card is de-activated. However, the NDA is perpetual and remains in effect even after a researcher or employee leaves. Such requirements are similar to those imposed upon non-commissioned civilian personnel in a police department.

A sample individual user data license agreement is shown in Figure 11-1. The sample document was developed by university contracting officers and lawyers in several institutions and government agencies. Most of the terms and conditions are applicable to national security projects that demand confidentiality.

11.3 Reaching Agreements among Partners

Federal, state, and local regulations require that agreements between agencies within their respective jurisdictions receive advance approval from their governing hierarchy. This precludes informal information sharing agreements between those agencies. We found that requirements varied from agency to agency according to the statutes by which they were governed.

For instance, the ordinances governing information sharing by the city of Tucson varied somewhat from those governing the city of Phoenix. This necessitated numerous attempts and passes at proposed documents by each city's law enforcement and legal staff before a final draft could be settled upon for approval by the city councils.

We found in general that similar language existed in the ordinances and statutes governing this exchange but the process varied significantly.

The [Agency] hereby grants access to the [Designated Data] data to the individual named below, hereinafter Licensee: [Name] [Organization] [Official mail address] [Telephone] [Facsimile] [Email]; subject to the following understandings, terms and conditions. These understandings, terms and conditions apply equally to all or to part of the data.

Permitted Uses:

- The information may only be used for research and development as described in the [Proposal Name] project (hereinafter referred to as *the proposal*).
- Summaries, analyses and interpretations of the properties of the data may be derived and used for research and development purposes.
- No excerpts of the data may be published in any context, or displayed to others except other Licensees with a signed Individual User Data License on file at [Agency] also bearing research and development responsibilities for the project described in the proposal.

Access to the Information:

- Access to the data is granted solely to the Licensee listed above for purposes of discharging his or her responsibilities of carrying out the research and development work described in the proposal.
- This license does not extend to other individuals within the Licensee's organization.
- The access is to be terminated on [End Date].

Indemnification:

- [Agency] shall not be liable in any way to the Licensee for any delays, inaccuracies, errors or omissions therefrom or in transmission or delivery of all or any part thereof or for any damages arising therefrom or occasioned thereby.
- In no event shall [Agency] be liable for any direct consequential, punitive, special or any other damages arising in any way from the availability of the service regardless of the form of action, whether contract or tort.

Delivery and Acceptance:

- Upon Licensee's execution of this Agreement, [Agency] shall deliver the data to Licensee.
- Licensee acknowledges and agrees that the data is licensed on an "as is with all defects" basis and is provided without maintenance, support or improvements. Accordingly, [Agency] shall not be required to make any corrections, or provide maintenance, or provide updates to Licensee, or assist Licensee in the understanding or use of the Database. No guarantee is made that the dictionary is adequately or completely described in the documentation.
- If [Agency] makes corrections or provides maintenance or updates to the data, [Agency] shall offer such corrections, maintenance and/or updates to Licensee.

Signed this __ day of ___, 20__   _____ (Licensee)

Figure 11-1. A Sample Individual User Data License.

Between [AGENCY 1] and [AGENCY 2]

WHEREAS, the real-time sharing of data and the development of tools may be essential for partners and for agencies and scientists who can assist in the development of such tools; and

WHEREAS, such interoperable multi-disciplinary data systems must incorporate appropriate protections to maintain confidentiality and scientific integrity of the data; and

Now therefore the parties hereto agree as follows:

I.   [AGENCY 1] and [AGENCY 2] will use collaborative efforts to develop a prototype model interoperable data system.

II. [AGENCY 1] and [AGENCY 2] will share data as permitted by the law of each state, respectively.

III. [AGENCY 1] and [AGENCY 2] will continue their current testing systems unless changes are required for state purposes.

IV. All parties shall own the data system design generated under this MOU subject to the rights of the federal government to use it as described in their funding agreement.

V.   The parties shall separately agree to more specific details regarding data elements to be used in the development of data systems models, which data elements can be confidentially and securely shared by [AGENCY 1] and [AGENCY 2] , and for any other data agreed upon by the parties, and the types of confidentiality restrictions that will apply to each.

VI. All data and information about the systems being developed will be kept confidential for five (5) years after termination of this agreement. The parties shall not disclose such Confidential Information except to each other. If such Confidential Information is disclosed to any party to this agreement or to its subcontractor, the party disclosing the information will assure that such disclosure shall be in writing and marked as Confidential Information. The parties agree to use such Confidential Information only for the purposes of this Agreement. The parties agree shall assure that its subcontractor agrees to keep all such Confidential Information confidential for five (5) years after the termination of this Agreement; provided that the receiving Party's obligations hereunder shall not apply to information that: (i) is or later becomes part of the public domain through no fault of the receiving Party; or, (ii) is received from a third party with no duty of confidentiality to the disclosing party; or, (iii) was developed independently by the receiving party prior to disclosure; or, (iv) is required to be disclosed by law or regulation. Any information that is transmitted orally or visually, in order to be protected hereunder, shall be identified as such by the disclosing party at the time of disclosure, and identified in writing to the receiving party, as Confidential Information as defined in this paragraph, within thirty (30) days after such oral or visual disclosure.

Figure 11-2. A Sample Memorandum of Understanding.

VII.   No data as described in paragraph II will be shared with a party outside this agreement without the expressed consent of the party providing the data. At the end of five (5) years after execution of this agreement, or the cancellation of this MOU, whichever comes sooner, such data will be provided back to the data originators and destroyed by other partners, unless the other partners are authorized in writing by the data originators to maintain the data.

VIII.   For the purposes of scientific publication and public release of detailed data, maps, and analyses, each MOU partner shall retain ownership and control of data it originated, and the data may not be provided by the other parties to any other agencies or individuals or utilized for analyses without the originator's consent. All parties to this MOU shall jointly own data analyses generated jointly under this MOU. No party shall publish or release the joint analyses conducted under this MOU without the review and approval of the other parties, unless otherwise required by law. Public posting of this information may be considered, depending on its usefulness and interest to the public and pending approval from the originating state. Press releases and press contacts shall be coordinated among the public affairs groups of each party.

IX.   All project personnel, whether or not employed, who receive systems data and information for use in this project shall sign individual Non-Disclosure Agreements.

X.   This agreement may only be amended in a writing signed by all parties.

XI.   This agreement shall be effective upon execution by all parties and shall remain effective until such time as it is cancelled by thirty days written notification by any of the parties to each of the others.

IN WITNESS WHEREOF, this Memorandum of Understanding has been duly executed by the parties hereto on the day and year appearing following their respective signatures.

[AGENCY 1]
    By: _____
    Title:
    Dated: _____/_____/_____

[AGENCY 2]
    By: _____
    Title:
    Dated: _____/_____/_____

It appears as though the size of the jurisdiction is proportional to the level of bureaucracy required. Our experience in developing an agreement between agencies in Arizona and agencies in California follows this premise.

Negotiating a contract between the University of Arizona and ARJIS (Automated Regional Justice Information System) of Southern California required six to nine months of discussion between legal staff, contract specialists, and agency officials. We are hopeful that many of the solutions to barriers in that process may be applied to the formation of formal agreements for information sharing with other agencies across state boundaries.

TPD has recently developed a generic Inter-Governmental Agreement (IGA) that could be adopted between different law enforcement agencies. This IGA was condensed from MOUs (Memorandum of Understanding), policies, and agreements that previously existed in various forms between numerous agencies. The IGA was drafted in a generic manner, including language from those laws, but excluding reference to any particular chapter or section. This allowed the required verbiage to exist in the document without being specific to any jurisdiction.

Sharing of information between agencies with disparate information systems has also led to bridging boundaries between software vendors and agencies (their customers). We took care not to violate licensing terms by insuring that non-disclosure agreements existed and that contract language assured compliance with the vendors' licensing policies.

We believe MOUs and IGAs can be used as templates of information sharing agreements and contracts, and can serve as a component of an ISI partnership framework. A sample MOU template is shown in Figure 11-2. Institutions and agencies are encouraged to freely adopt and modify this template for their purposes.

11.4   The COPLINK Chronicle

We include below a chronicle of funding, research and development, and media reports of relevance to our COPLINK project. Many agencies, partners, and individuals have contributed significantly to the success of this program, which has grown from its humble academic research roots to widespread deployment and impact in public safety and homeland security.

The COPLINK system, which has been cited as a national model for public safety information sharing and analysis, has been adopted in more than 100 law enforcement and intelligence agencies. The COPLINK research had been featured in the *New York Times, Newsweek, Los Angeles Times, Washington Post,* and *Boston Globe,* among others. The COPLINK project was selected as a finalist in 2003 for the prestigious International

Association of Chiefs of Police (IACP)/Motorola 2003 Webber Seavey Award for Quality in Law Enforcement. COPLINK research has recently been expanded to border protection (BorderSafe), disease and bioagent surveillance (BioPortal), and terrorism informatics research (Dark Web), funded by the NSF, CIA, and DHS.

- September 1994-August 1998, NSF/ARPA/NASA, Digital Library Initiative (DLI) funding: Selected concept association and data mining techniques developed under the DLI program.

- July 1997-January 2000, DOJ, National Institute of Justice (NIJ) funding: Initial COPLINK research -- database integration and access for a law enforcement Intranet.

- January 2000, first COPLINK prototype: Developed and tested in the Tucson Police Department.

- May 2000, Knowledge Computing Corporation (KCC) founded: KCC received venture capital funding and licensed COPLINK technology.

- January 7, 2001, Arizona Daily Star: "Technology developed in Tucson is helping police catch criminals faster. COPLINK products let police agencies rapidly share crime information across jurisdictional line."

- July 2001, POLICE magazine: "COPLINK shifts and shares information – fast."

- October 23, 2002, Tucson Citizen: "Tucson cops, local software to help in D.C. sniper probe."

- November 2, 2002, New York Times: "An electronic cop that plays hunches." COPLINK was used to assist in the Washington, D.C. sniper investigation.

- November 7, 2002, Washington Post: "A missing link most wanted."

- November 18, 2002, Life Week magazine (Chinese): "A Sherlock Holmes for the Internet age."

- January, 2003, Public Technology: "COPLINK project receives the PTI Technology Award."

- March 3, 2003, Newsweek magazine: "A Google for cops."

- April 15, 2003, ABC News: "Google for cops."

- July 17, 2003, Boston Globe: "Software helps police draw crime links."

- August 19, 2003, Dodge City Daily Globe: "Northwest Kansas law enforcement to use program to sift through records."

- December 3, 2003, Motorola.com: "Tucson Police Department's COPLINK project was named a finalist of the prestigious Webber Seavey Award for quality in law enforcement."

- December 6, 2003, Los Angeles Daily News: "Cops can hit the links soon. New search engine would catalog, interpret data for investigations."

- September 2003-August 2005, NSF, DHS, CNRI funding for BorderSafe project: Cross-jurisdictional information sharing and criminal network analysis.

- September 2003-August 2006, NSF, Digital Government Program funding for Dark Web project: Social network analysis and identity deception detection for law enforcement and homeland security.

- August 2004-July 2008, NSF, Information Technology Research (ITR) Program funding for BioPortal: A national center of excellence for infectious disease informatics.

11.5   Future Directions

Forming a sustainable, win-win collaboration partnership between academics and selected law enforcement or intelligence agencies is difficult and, yet, potentially fruitful. In our COPLINK experience, we have seen that such a collaboration bears fruits in scientific innovation and social impact. We believe that we have made significant contributions to information sharing, crime data mining, deception detection, criminal network analysis, and disease surveillance research. We have also witnessed, first-hand, criminals arrested and lives saved as a result of public safety agencies using our technologies.

In the next decade, we envision significant breakthroughs in several areas. The BorderSafe project will continue to contribute to border safety and cross-jurisdictional criminal network analysis research. The Dark Web project will help create an invaluable terrorism research testbed and develop advanced terrorism analysis methods. The BioPortal project will contribute to the development of a national or even international infectious disease and bioagent information sharing and analysis system.

11.6 Questions for Discussion

1. How can you identify law enforcement and security agencies in your neighborhood or city that are interested in collaborating with you?

2. What are some ways to create a research lab that can handle potentially sensitive and confidential information? What are the roles and obligations of research scientists and students?

3. How do you work with university contracting and legal offices to develop the memorandum, license, and agreement for partnering agencies?

4. What are some ways to deliver immediate values to the partnering agencies during a research process?

Chapter 12

CONCLUSIONS AND FUTURE DIRECTIONS

In this book, we discuss technical issues regarding intelligence and security informatics (ISI) research to accomplish the critical missions of national security. We propose a research framework addressing the technical challenges facing counter-terrorism and crime-fighting applications with a primary focus on the knowledge discovery from databases (KDD) perspective. We identify and incorporate in the framework six classes of ISI technologies: information sharing and collaboration, crime association mining, crime classification and clustering, intelligence text mining, spatial and temporal analysis of crime patterns, and criminal network analysis. We also present a set of COPLINK case studies, ranging from detection of criminal identity deception to intelligent web portals for monitoring terrorist web sites, demonstrating the potential of ISI technologies in contributing to the critical missions of national security.

As this new ISI discipline continues to evolve and advance, several important directions need to be pursued, including technology development, testbed creation, and social, organizational, and policy studies.

- New technologies need to be developed and many existing information technologies should be re-examined and adapted for national security applications. The knowledge discovery perspective provides a promising direction. However, new technologies should be developed in a legal and ethical framework without compromising the privacy or civil liberties of citizens.

- Large-scale, non-sensitive data testbeds consisting of data from diverse, authoritative, and open sources and in different formats should be created and made available to the ISI research community. Lack of real research data has been a long-standing problem in intelligence- and security-related research. Many researchers are forced to use simulated or synthetic data that may not resemble true crime data characteristics. Furthermore, comparing competing technical approaches has been difficult because of the lack of standard testing collections. A comprehensive and non-sensitive open source data collection, analogous to the MUC (Message Understanding Conference) collection, will be of great value for ISI researchers to experiment with, test, and evaluate various technologies, and to compare and share findings, insights, and knowledge. Advanced methods may need to be employed to scrub data contained in the non-open source testbed to ensure data confidentiality while preserving its characteristics and underlying structures.

- The ultimate goal of ISI research is to enhance our national security. However, the question of how this type of research has impacted and will impact society, organizations, and the general public remains unanswered. Researchers from social sciences, political sciences, organizational and management sciences, psychology, and education may contribute substantially to this aspect.

We hope active ISI research will help improve knowledge discovery and dissemination and enhance information sharing and collaboration among academics, local, state, and federal agencies, and industry, thereby bringing positive impacts to all aspects of our society.

ACKNOWLEDGEMENTS

We would like to acknowledge the funding support of many federal agencies over the past decade and the invaluable contributions from our research partners.

Research Partners

We thank our research partners, who have contributed significantly to the projects reported in the case studies.

- Tucson Police Department
- Phoenix Police Department
- Pima County Sheriff's Department
- Tucson Customs and Border Protection
- San Diego, Automated Regional Justice Information Systems (ARJIS)
- Corporation for National Research Initiatives (CNRI)
- California Department of Health Services
- New York State Department of Health
- United States Geological Survey
- Library of Congress
- San Diego Supercomputer Center (SDSC)
- National Center for Supercomputing Research (NCSA)

Funding Support

The projects reported in the case studies have been mainly funded by the following grants:

- NSF/CIA, Knowledge Discovery and Dissemination (KDD) Program, "Detecting Identity Concealment," September 2004-August 2005.
- NSF, Information Technology Research (ITR) Program, "A National Center of Excellence for Infectious Disease Informatics," IIS-0428241, August 2004-July 2008.

- NSF, Digital Government Program, "COPLINK Center: Social Network Analysis and Identity Deception Detection for Law Enforcement and Homeland Security," IIS-0429364, September 2003-August 2006.

- DHS, Corporation for National Research Initiatives (CNRI), "BorderSafe Initiative Phase-2," June 2004-March 2005.

- DHS, CNRI, "BorderSafe Initiative," October 2003-September 2004.

- NSF, Information Technology Research (ITR) Program, "COPLINK Center for Intelligence and Security Informatics – A Crime Data Mining Approach to Developing Border Safe Research," EIA-0326348, September 2003-August 2005.

- NSF/CIA KDD Program, "ARJIS/COPLINK Border Safe Research and Testbed," EIA-9983304, March 2003-March 2004.

- NSF, Information Technology Research (ITR) Program, "Developing a Collaborative Information and Knowledge Management Infrastructure," IIS-0114011, 2001-2004.

- NSF, "Developing a National Infectious Disease Information Infrastructure: An Experiment in West Nile Virus and Botulism," EIA-9983304, October 2003-March 2004.

- NSF, Digital Government Program, "COPLINK Center: Information and Knowledge Management for Law Enforcement," EAI-9983304, July, 2000-March, 2004.

- NSF, "Workshop: Symposium on Intelligence and Security Informatics," EIA-0317269, March 2003-December 2003.

- NSF/CIA, KDD Program, "COPLINK Testbed for Homeland Security Data Mining," September 2002-June 2003.

- Digital Equipment Corporation, External Technology Grants Program, "COPLINK: Database Integration and Access for a Law Enforcement Intranet," DEC AlphaServer 4100, 1997-2001.

- City of Tucson, "Coplink Concept Space: An Intelligence Analysis Tool," January-September, 2000.

- Silicon Graphics Inc. (SGI), SGI Origin2000 supercomputer, 1998-2001.

- DOD, Advanced Research Projects Agency (DARPA), "The Interspace Prototype: An Analysis Environment based on Scalable Semantics," June 1997-May 2001.

- DOJ, National Institute of Justice, "COPLINK: Database Integration and Access for a Law Enforcement Intranet," July 1997-January 2000.

- DOD, Advanced Research Projects Agency (DARPA), "GeoWorlds, Task 5.1 Under Dasher," June 1998-December 1998.

- NSF/ARPA/NASA, Digital Library Initiative, "Building the Interspace: Digital Library Infrastructure for a University Engineering Community," IRI9411318, September 1994-August 1998.

REFERENCES

Adderley, R. and Musgrove, P. B. (2001). Data mining case study: Modeling the behavior of offenders who commit serious sexual assaults. In F. Provost and R. Srikant (Eds.), *Proceedings of the 7th ACM SIGKDD International Conference on Knowledge Discovery and Data Mining* (pp. 215-220). New York: Association for Computing Machinery.

Agrawal, R., Imielinski, T., and Swami, A. (1993). Mining association rules between sets of items in large databases. In S. Jajodia and P. Buneman (Eds.), *Proceedings of the ACM SIGMOD International Conference on Management of Data* (pp. 207-216). New York: Association for Computing Machinery.

Albert, R. and Barabasi, A.-L. (2002). Statistical mechanics of complex networks. *Reviews of Modern Physics, 74*(1), 47-97.

Aleskerov, E., Freisleben, B., and Rao, B. (1997). CARDWATCH: A neural network based database mining system for credit card fraud detection. In *Proceedings of Computational Intelligence for Financial Engineering (CIFE)* (pp. 220-226). Piscataway, NJ: IEEE.

Al-Fedaghi, Sabah S. and Al-Anzi, F. (1989) A new algorithm to generate Arabic root-pattern forms. In *Proceedings of the 11th National Computer Conference*, King Fahd University of Petroleum and Minerals, Dhahran, Saudi Arabia, (pp. 4-7).

American Civil Liberties Union. (2004). *MATRIX: Myths and reality*. Retrieved July 27, 2004, from the World Wide Web:
http://www.aclu.org/Privacy/Privacy.cfm?ID=14894&c=130

Anderberg, M. R. (1973). *Cluster Analysis for Applications*. New York: Academic Press.

Anderson, T., Arbetter, L., Benawides, A., and Longmore-Etheridge, A. (1994). Security works. *Security Management, 38*(17), 17-20.

Arabie, P., Boorman, S. A., and Levitt, P. R. (1978). Constructing blockmodels: How and why. *Journal of Mathematical Psychology, 17*, 21-63.

Arquilla, J. and Ronfeldt, D. F. Advent of Netwar. (1996). *Rand Report*, http://www.rand.org/

Badiru, A. B., Karasz, J. M., and Holloway, B. T. (1988). AREST: Armed Robbery Eidetic Suspect Typing expert system. *Journal of Police Science and Administration, 16*, 210-216.

Baker, W. E. and Faulkner, R. R. (1993). The social organization of conspiracy: Illegal networks in the heavy electrical equipment industry. *American Sociological Review, 58*(12), 837-860.

Baluja, S., Mittal, V., and Sukthankar, R. (1999). Applying machine learning for high performance named-entity extraction. In N. Cercone, K. Naruedomkul and K. Kogure (Eds.), *PACLING '99: Proceedings of the Conference (Pacific Association of Computational Linguistics)* (pp. 1-14). Waterloo, Ont.: Dept. of Computer Science, University of Waterloo.

Bell, G. S. and Sethi, A. (2001). Matching records in a national medical patient index. *Communications of the ACM, 44*(9), 83-88.

Berndt, D. J., Bhat, S., Fisher, J. W., Hevner, A. R., and Studnicki, J. (2004). Data analytics for bioterrorism surveillance. In H. Chen, R. Moore, D. Zeng and J. Leavitt (Eds.), *Proceedings of the Second Symposium on Intelligence and Security Informatics (ISI'04)* (pp.17-28). Berlin: Springer.

Berndt, D. J., Hevner, A. R., and Studnicki, J. (2003). Bioterrorism surveillance with real-time data warehousing. In H. Chen, R. Miranda, D. Zeng, C. Demchak, et al. (Eds.), *Proceedings of the First NSF/NIJ Symposium on Intelligence and Security Informatics (ISI'03)* (pp. 322-335). Berlin: Springer.

Borthwick, A., Sterling, J., Agichtein, E., and Grishman, R. (1998). NYU: Description of the MENE named entity system as used in MUC-7. In *Proceedings of the 7th Message Understanding Conference (MUC-7).*

Bowen, J. E. (1994). An expert system for police investigators of economic crimes. *Expert Systems with Applications, 7*(2), 235-248.

Brahan, J. W., Lam, K. P., Chan, H., and Leung, W. (1998). AICAMS: Artificial Intelligence Crime Analysis and Management System. *Knowledge-Based Systems, 11*, 355-361.

Brantingham, P. and Brantingham, P. (1981). *Environmental Criminology.* Beverly Hills: Sage.

Brown, D. E. (1998a). The Regional Crime Analysis Program (RECAP): A framework for mining data to catch criminals. In F. DiCesare, M. Jafari, and M. Zhou (Eds.), *Proceedings of the 1998 International Conference on Systems, Man, and Cybernetics* (vol. 3, pp. 2848-2853). Piscataway, NJ: IEEE.

Brown, D. E., Dalton, J., and Hoyle, H. (2004). Spatial forecast methods for terrorism events in urban environments. In H. Chen, R. Moore, D. Zeng and J. Leavitt (Eds.), *Proceedings of the Second Symposium on Intelligence and Security Informatics (ISI'04)* (pp. 426-435). Berlin: Springer.

Brown, D. E. and Hagen, S. (2002). Data association methods with applications to law enforcement. *Decision Support Systems, 34*(4), 369-378.

Brown, D. E. and Oxford, R. B. (2001). Data mining time series with applications to crime analysis. In T. Bahill and F.-Y. Wang (Eds.), *Proceedings of the 2001 IEEE International Conference on Systems, Man and Cybernetics Conference* (vol. 3, pp. 1453-1458). Piscataway, NJ: IEEE.

Brown, M. (1998b). *Future Alert Contact Network: Reducing crime via early notification.* Retrieved July 27, 2004, from the World Wide Web: http://pti.nw.dc.us/solutions/solutions98/public_safety/charlotte.html

Buccella, A., Cechich, A., and Brisaboa, N. R. (2003). An ontology approach to data integration. *Journal of Computer Science and Technology, 3*(2), 62-68.

Buetow, T., Chaboya, L., O'Toole, C., Cushna, T., Daspit, D., Peterson, T., et al. (2003). A spatial temporal visualizer for law enforcement. In H. Chen, R. Miranda, D. Zeng, C. Demchak, et al. (Eds.), *Proceedings of the First NSF/NIJ Symposium on Intelligence and Security Informatics (ISI'03)* (pp. 181-193). Berlin: Springer.

Burt, R. S. (1976). Positions in networks. *Social Forces, 55*, 93-122.

Carley, K. M., Dombroski, M., Tsvetovat, M., Reminga, J., and Kamneva, N. (2003). Destabilizing dynamic covert networks. In *Proceedings of the 8th International Command and Control Research and Technology Symposium.*

Carley, K. M., Lee, J., and Krackhardt, D. (2002). Destabilizing networks. *Connections, 24*(3), 79-92.

Chan, P. K. and Stolfo, S. J. (1998). Toward scalable learning with non-uniform class and cost distributions: A case study in credit card fraud detection. In R. Agrawal and P. Stolorz (Eds.), *Proceedings of the 4th International Conference on Knowledge Discovery and Data Mining (KDD 98)* (pp. 164-168). Menlo Park, Calif.: AAAI Press.

Chau, M., Xu, J., and Chen, H. (2002). Extracting meaningful entities from police narrative reports. *Proceedings of the National Conference on Digital Government Research.*

Chen, H. (2001) *Knowledge Management Systems: A Text Mining Perspective.* Tucson, AZ: The University of Arizona.

Chen, H., Chung, W., Xu, J., Wang, G., Chau, M., and Qin, Y. (2004a). Crime data mining: A general framework and some examples. *IEEE Computer, 37*(4), 50-56.

Chen, H., Fuller, S. S., Friedman, C., and Hersh, W. (Eds.) (2005). *Medical Informatics: Knowledge Management and Data Mining in Biomedicine.* Berlin: Springer.

Chen, H., Houston, A. L., Sewell, R. R., and Schatz, B. R. (1998). Internet browsing and searching: User evaluation of category map and concept space techniques. *Journal of the American Society for Information Science, 49*(7), 582-603.

Chen, H. and Lynch, K. J. (1992). Automatic construction of networks of concepts characterizing document databases. *IEEE Transactions on Systems, Man and Cybernetics, 22*(5), 885-902.

Chen, H., Miranda, R., Zeng, D., Demchak, C., Schroeder, J., and Madhusudan, T. (Eds.). (2003a). *Intelligence and Security Informatics: Proceedings of the First NSF/NIJ Symposium on Intelligence and Security Informatics.* Berlin: Springer.

Chen, H., Moore, R., Zeng, D., and Leavitt, J. (Eds.). (2004b). *Intelligence and Security Informatics: Proceedings of the Second Symposium on Intelligence and Security Informatics.* Berlin: Springer.

Chen, H., Qin, J., Reid, E., Chung, W., Zhou, Y., Xi, W., et al. (2004c). The Dark Web Portal: Collecting and analyzing the presence of domestic and international terrorist groups on the Web. In *Proceedings of the 7th Annual IEEE Conference on Intelligent Transportation Systems (ITSC 2004).*

Chen, H., Schroeder, J., Hauck, R., Ridgeway, L., Atabakhsh, H., Gupta, H., et al. (2003b). COPLINK Connect: Information and knowledge management for law enforcement. *Decision Support Systems, 34*(3), 271-285.

Chen, H., Schuffels, C., and Orwig, R. (1996). Internet categorization and search: A self-organizing approach. *Journal of Visual Communication and Image Representation, 7*(1), 88-102.

Chen, H., Zeng, D., Atabakhsh, H., Wyzga, W., and Schroeder, J. (2003c). COPLINK: Managing law enforcement data and knowledge. *Communications of the ACM, 46*(1), 28-34.

Chen, H., Wang, F. Y., and Zeng, D. (2004). Intelligence and security informatics for homeland security: information, communication, and transportation. *IEEE Transactions on Intelligent Transportation Systems, 5*(4), 329-341.

Chen, H. and Xu, J. (2005) Intelligence and security informatics for national security: A knowledge discovery perspective. In B. Cronin (Ed.), *Annual Review of Information Science and Technology (ARIST),* Volume 40. Information Today, Inc., Medford, New Jersey.

Chen, I.-M. A. and Rotem, D. (1998). Integrating information from multiple independently developed data sources. In K. Makki and L. Bouganim, (Eds.), *Proceedings of the 7th International Conference on Information and Knowledge Management* (pp. 242-250). New York: Association for Computing Machinery.

Chinchor, N. A. (1998). Overview of MUC-7/MET-2. In *Proceedings of the 7th Message Understanding Conference (MUC-7).*

Coady, W. F. (1985). Automated link analysis: Artificial intelligence-based tool for investigators. *Police Chief, 52*(9), 22-23.

Collins, P. I., Johnson, G. F., Choy, A., Davidson, K. T., and Mackay, R. E. (1998). Advances in violent crime analysis and law enforcement: The Canadian Violent Crime Linkage Analysis System. *Journal of Government Information, 25*(3), 277-284.

Cook, J. S. and Cook, L. L. (2003). Social, ethical and legal issues of data mining. In J. Wang (Ed.), *Data mining: Opportunities and Challenges* (pp. 395-420). Hershey, PA: Idea Group Publishing.

Craglia, M., Haining, R., and Wiles, P. (2000). A comparative evaluation of approaches to urban crime pattern analysis. *Urban Studies, 37*(4), 711-729.

Cristianini, N. and Shawe-Taylor, J. (2000). *An Introduction to Support Vector Machines: And Other Kernel-based Learning Methods.* New York: Cambridge University Press.

Damianos, L., Ponte, J., Wohlever, S., Reeder, F., Day, D., Wilson, G., et al. (2002). MiTAP for bio-security: A case study. *AI Magazine, 23*(4), 13-29.

de Vel, O., Anderson, A., Corney, M., and Mohay, G. (2001). Mining e-mail content for author identification forensics. *SIGMOD Record, 30*(4), 55-64.

Defays, D. (1977). An efficient algorithm for a complete link method. *Computer Journal, 20*(4), 364-366.

Demchak, C., Friis, C., and La Porte, T. M. (2000). Webbing governance: national differences in constructing the face of public organizations. In G. David Garson (Ed.), *Handbook of Public Information Systems*. New York: Marcel Dekker.

Diederich, J., Kindermann, J., Leopold, E., and Paass, G. (2000). Authorship attribution with support vector machines. *Applied Intelligence, 19*(1-2), 109-123.

Dolotov, A. and Strickler, M. (2003). Web-based intelligence reports system.. In H. Chen, R. Miranda, D. Zeng, C. Demchak, et al. (Eds.), *Proceedings of the First NSF/NIJ Symposium on Intelligence and Security Informatics (ISI'03)* (pp. 39-58). Berlin: Springer.

Duda, R. O. and Hart, P. E. (1973). *Pattern recognition and scene analysis*. New York: Wiley.

Eisen, M. B., Spellman, P. T., Brown, P. O., and Botstein, D. (1998). Cluster analysis and display of genome-wide expression patterns. *Proceedings of the National Academy of Sciences, 95*(25), 14863-14868.

Eisenbeis, R. and Avery, R. (1972). *Discrimination Analysis and Classification Procedures*. Lanham, MA: Lexington Books.

Elison, W. (2000) Netwar: Studying rebels on the Internet. *The Social Studies* 91, 127-131.

Estivill-Castro, V. and Lee, I. (2001). Data mining techniques for autonomous exploration of large volumes of geo-referenced crime data. In *Proceedings of the 6th International Conference on GeoComputation*.

Evan, W. M. (1972). An organization-set model of interorganizational relations. In M. Tuite, R. Chisholm and M. Radnor (Eds.), *Interorganizational decision-making* (pp. 181-200). Chicago: Aldine.

Faggiani, D. and McLaughlin, C. (1999). Using nation incident-based reporting system data for strategic crime analysis. *Journal of Quantitative Criminology, 15*(2), 181-191.

Fayyad, U. M., Djorgovshi, S. G., and Weir, N. (1996). Automating the analysis and cataloging of sky surveys. In U. Fayyad, G. Piatetsky-Shapiro, P. Smyth and R. Uthurusamy (Eds.), *Advances in Knowledge Discovery and Data Mining* (pp. 471-493). Menlo Park, CA: AAAI Press.

Fayyad, U. M. and Uthurusamy, R. (2002). Evolving data mining into solutions for insights. *Communications of the ACM, 45*(8), 28-31.

Federal Bureau of Investigation. (1992). *Uniform Crime Reporting Handbook: National Incident-based Reporting System (NIBRS)*. Washington, D.C.: The Bureau.

Freeman, L. C. (1979). Centrality in social networks: Conceptual clarification. *Social Networks, 1*, 215-240.

Garcia-Molina, H., Ullman, J. D., and Widom, J. (2002). *Database Systems: The Complete Book*. Upper Saddle River, NJ: Prentice-Hall.

Getis, A. and Ord, J. K. (1992). The analysis of spatial association by use of distance statistics. *Geographical Analysis, 24*, 189-199.

Gibson, D., Kleinberg, J., and Raghavan, P. (1998). Inferring Web communities from link topology. In R. Akscyn, D. McCracken, and E. Yoder (Eds.), *Proceedings of the 9th ACM Conference on Hypertext and Hypermedia* (pp. 225-234). New York: Association for Computing Machinery.

Goldberg, D., Nichols, D., Oki, B., and Terry, D. (1992). Using collaborative filtering to weave an information tapestry. *Communications of the ACM, 35*(12), 61-69.

Goldberg, H. G. and Senator, T. E. (1998). Restructuring databases for knowledge discovery by consolidation and link formation. In D. Jensen and H. Goldberg (Eds.), *Proceedings of the 1998 AAAI Fall Symposium on Artificial Intelligence and Link Analysis* (pp. 47-52). Menlo Park, CA: AAAI Press.

Goldberg, H. G. and Wong, R. W. H. (1998). Restructuring transactional data for link analysis in the FinCen AI System. In D. Jensen and H. Goldberg (Eds.), *Proceedings of the 1998 AAAI Fall Symposium on Artificial Intelligence and Link Analysis* (pp. 38-46). Menlo Park, CA: AAAI Press.

Grishman, R. (2003). Information extraction. In R. Mitkov (Ed.), *The Oxford Handbook of Computational Linguistics* (pp. 545-559). New York: Oxford University Press.

Grubesic, T. H. and Murray, A. T. (2001). Detecting hot spots using cluster analysis and GIS. In *Proceedings of 2001 Crime Mapping Research Conference*.

Haas, L. M. (2002). Data integration through database federation. *IBM Systems Journal, 41*(4), 578-596.

Han, J. and Kamber, M. (2001). *Data Mining: Concepts and Techniques.* San Francisco, CA: Morgan Kaufmann.

Hand, D. J. (1981). *Discrimination and Classification.* Chichester, U.K.: Wiley.

Harris, K. D. (1990). *Geographic Factors in Policing.* New York: McGraw-Hill.

Hasselbring, W. (2000). Information system integration. *Communications of the ACM, 43*(6), 33-38.

Hassibi, K. (2000). Detecting payment card fraud with neural networks. In P. J. G. Lisboa, A. Vellido and B. Edisbury (Eds.), *Business Applications of Neural Networks.* Singapore: World Scientific.

Hauck, R. V., Atabakhsh, H., Ongvasith, P., Gupta, H., and Chen, H. (2002). Using COPLINK to analyze criminal justice data. *IEEE Computer, 35*(3), 30-37.

Heckerman, D. (1995). A tutorial on learning with Bayesian networks. In M. Jordan (Ed.), *Learning in Graphical Models* (pp. 301-354). Cambridge, MA: MIT Press. (Also available as Research Report No. MSR-TR-95-06 from Microsoft).

Hsu, C. W. and Lin, C. J. (2002). A comparison of methods for multi-class support vector machines. *IEEE Transactions on Neural Networks, 13*, 415-425.

Hummon, N. P. (2000) Utility and dynamic social networks. *Social Networks 22*, 221-249.

Jain, A. K. and Flynn, P. J. (1996). Image segmentation using clustering. In N. Ahuja and K. Bowyer (Eds.), *Advances in Image Understanding* (pp. 65-83). Piscataway, NJ: IEEE Press.

Jain, A. K., Murty, M. N., and Flynn, P. J. (1999). Data clustering: A review. *ACM Computing Surveys, 31*(3), 264-323.

Jhingran, A. D., Mattos, N., and Pirahesh, H. (2002). Information integration: A research agenda. *IBM Systems Journal, 41*(4), 555-562.

Kangas, L. J., Terrones, K. M., Keppel, R. D., and La Moria, R. D. (2003). Computer Aided Tracking and Characterization of Homicides and sexual assaults (CATCH). In J. Mena (Ed.), *Investigative Data Mining for Security and Criminal Detection* (pp. 364-375). Amsterdam: Butterworth Heinemann.

Kay, B. A., Timperi, R. J., Morse, S. S., Forslund, D., McGowan, J. J., and O'Brien, T. (1998). Innovative information-sharing strategies. *Emerging Infectious Diseases, 4*(3).

Kennedy, L.W. and Lunn, C.M. (2003). Developing a Foundation for Policy Relevant Terrorism Research in Criminology. *(Progress Report 1),* http://www.andromeda.rutgers.edu/~rcst/PDFFiles/ProgressReport.doc

Klerks, P. (2001). The network paradigm applied to criminal organizations: Theoretical nitpicking or a relevant doctrine for investigators? Recent developments in the Netherlands. *Connections, 24*(3), 53-65.

Kohonen, T. (1995). *Self-organizing Maps.* Berlin: Springer-Verlag.

Koperski, K. and Han, J. (1995). Discovery of spatial association rules in geographic information databases. In M. J. Egenhofer and J. R. Herring, *Proceedings of the 4th International Symposium on Large Spatial Databases (Advances in Spatial Databases)* (pp. 47-66). New York: Springer-Verlag.

Krebs, V. E. (2001). Mapping networks of terrorist cells. *Connections, 24*(3), 43-52.

Krupka, G. R. and Hausman, K. (1998). IsoQuest Inc.: Description of the NetOwl text extractor system as used for MUC-7. In *Proceedings of the 7th Message Understanding Conference (MUC-7).*

Kumar, A. and Olmeda, I. (1999). A study of composite or hybrid classifiers for knowledge discovery. *INFORMS Journal on Computing, 11*(3), 267-277.

Lee, R. (1998). Automatic information extraction from documents: A tool for intelligence and law enforcement analysts. In *Proceedings of the 1998 AAAI Fall Symposium on Artificial Intelligence and Link Analysis* (pp. 63-67). Menlo Park, CA: AAAI Press.

Lee, W. and Stolfo, S. (1998). Data mining approaches for intrusion detection. In *Proceedings of the 7th USENIX Security Symposium.*

Levenshtein, V. L. (1966). Binary codes capable of correcting deletions, insertions, and reversals. *Soviet Physics Doklady, 10*, 707-710.

Levine, N. (2000). CrimeStat: A spatial statistics program for the analysis of crime incident locations. *Crime Mapping News (2)*1, 8-9.

Li, J., Zheng, R., and Chen, H. (forthcoming). From fingerprint to writeprint. *Communications of the ACM.*

Lim, E.-P., Srivastava, J., Prabhakar, S., and Richardson, J. (1996). Entity identification in database integration. *Information Sciences, 89*, 1-38.

Lin, S. and Brown, D. E. (2003). Criminal incident data association using the OLAP technology. In H. Chen, R. Miranda, D. Zeng, C. Demchak, et al. (Eds.), *Proceedings of the First NSF/NIJ Symposium on Intelligence and Security Informatics (ISI'03)* (pp. 13-26). Berlin: Springer.

Lippmann, R. P. (1987). An introduction to computing with neural networks. *IEEE Acoustics Speech and Signal Processing Magazine, 4*(2), 4-22.

Liu, H. and Motoda, H. (1998). *Feature Selection for Knowledge Discovery and Data Mining.* Norwell, MA: Kluwer Academic Publishers.

Lorrain, F. P. and White, H. C. (1971). Structural equivalence of individuals in social networks. *Journal of Mathematical Sociology, 1*, 49-80.

Lu, Q., Huang, Y., and Shekhar, S. (2003). Evacuation planning: A capacity constrained routing approach. In H. Chen, R. Miranda, D. Zeng, C. Demchak, et al. (Eds.), *Proceedings of the First NSF/NIJ Symposium on Intelligence and Security Informatics (ISI'03)* (pp. 111-125). Berlin: Springer.

Mannila, H., Toivonen, H., and I., V. A. (1994). Efficient algorithms for discovering association rules. In U. M. Fayyad and R. Uthurusamy (Eds.), *Proceedings of Knowledge Discovery in Databases (KDD'94)* (pp. 181-192). Menlo Park, CA: AAAI Press.

Marshall, B., Kaza, S., Xu, J., Atabakhsh, H., Petersen, T., Violette, C., et al. (2004). Cross-jurisdictional criminal activity networks to support border and transportation security. *Proceedings of the 7th Annual IEEE Conference on Intelligent Transportation Systems (ITSC 2004)*, Washington, D.C.

McAndrew, D. (1999). The structural analysis of criminal networks. In D. Canter and L. Alison (Eds), *The Social Psychology of Crime: Groups, Teams, and Networks, Offender Profiling Series* (pp. 53-94). Dartmouth: Aldershot.

McDonald, D. and Chen, H. (2002). Using sentence-selection heuristics to rank text segments in TXTRACTOR. In G. Marchionini and W. R. Hersh (Eds.), *Proceedings of the Second ACM/IEEE-CS Joint Conference on Digital Libraries (JCDL'02)* (pp. 28-35). New York: Association for Computing Machinery.

McFadden, D. (1973). Conditional logit analysis of qualitative choice behavior. In P. Zarembka, (Ed.), *Frontiers of Econometrics* (pp. 105-142). New York: Academic Press.

McKeown, K., Barzilay, R.,, et al. (2003). Columbia's Newsblaster: New features and future directions. In *Proceedings of Human Language Technology Conference (HLT-NAACL 2003)*(pp. 15-16), Edmonton, Canada.

Mena, J. (2003). *Investigative Data Mining for Security and Criminal Detection.* Amsterdam, Holland: Butterworth Heinemann.

Miller, S., Crystal, M., Fox, H., Ramshaw, L., Schwartz, R., Stone, R., et al. (1998). BBN: Description of the SIFT system as used for MUC-7. In *Proceedings of the 7th Message Understanding Conference (MUC-7)*.

Moore, R. and Gibbs, G. (2002). Emile: Using a chatbot conversation to enhance the learning of social theory. Univ. of Huddersfield, Huddersfield, England.

Moran, P. A. P. (1950). Notes on continuous stochastic phenomena. *Biometrika, 37*, 17-23.

Murray, A. T. and Estivill-Castro, V. (1998). Cluster discovery techniques for exploratory spatial data analysis. *International Journal of Geographical Information Science, 12*, 431-443.

Murray, A. T., McGuffog, I., Western, J. S., and Mullins, P. (2001). Exploratory spatial data analysis techniques for examining urban crime. *British Journal of Criminology, 41*, 309-329.

National Research Council. (2002). *Making the Nation Safer: The Role of Science and Technology in Countering Terrorism.* Washington, DC: National Academy Press.

Newcombe, H. B. et al. (1959). Automatic linkage of vital records. *Science, 130*(3381), 954-959.

Office of Homeland Security. (2002). *National Strategy for Homeland Security.* Washington D.C.: Office of Homeland Security.

O'Hara, C. E. and O'Hara, G. L. (1980). *Fundamentals of Criminal Investigation* (5th ed.). Springfield, IL: Charles C. Thomas.

O'Harrow, R. (2005). *No Place to Hide.* New York: Free Press.

Ord, J. K. and Getis, A. (1995). Local spatial autocorrelation statistics: Distributional issues and an application. *Geographical Analysis, 27*, 286-296.

Patman, F. and Thompson, P. (2003). Names: A new frontier in text mining. In H. Chen, R. Miranda, D. Zeng, C. Demchak, et al. (Eds.), *Proceedings of the First NSF/NIJ Symposium on Intelligence and Security Informatics (ISI'03)* (pp. 27-38). Berlin: Springer.

Peng, F., Schuurmans, D., Keselj, V., and Wang, S. (2003). Automated authorship attribution with character level language models. Paper presented at the 10th Conference of the European Chapter of the Association for Computational Linguistics.

Pinner, R. W., Rebmann, C. A., Schuchat, A., and Hughes, J. M. (2003). Disease surveillance and the academic, clinical, and public health communities. *Emerging Infectious Diseases, 9*(7).

Quinlan, J. R. (1986). Introduction of decision trees. *Machine Learning, 1*, 86-106.

Quinlan, J. R. (1993). *C4.5: Programs for Machine Learning.* Morgan Kaufmann.

Raghu, T. S., Ramesh, R., and Whinston, A. B. (2003). Addressing the homeland security problem: A collaborative decision-making framework. In H. Chen, R. Miranda, D. Zeng, C. Demchak, et al. (Eds.), *Proceedings of the First NSF/NIJ Symposium on Intelligence and Security Informatics (ISI'03)* (pp. 249-265). Berlin: Springer.

Rahm, E. and Bernstein, P. A. (2001). A survey of approaches to automatic schema matching. *The VLDB Journal, 10,* 334-350.

Rasmussen, E. (1992). Clustering algorithms. In W. B. Frakes and R. Baeza-Yates (Eds.), *Information Retrieval: Data Structures and Algorithms* (pp. 419-442). Englewood Cliffs, NJ: Prentice Hall.

Reid, E. O. F. (1997). Evolution of a body of knowledge: an analysis of terrorism research. *Information Processing and Management 33,* 91-106.

Reid, E. O. F., and Chen, H. (forthcoming). Contemporary terrorism researchers' patterns of collaboration and influence. *Journal of the American Society for Information Science and Technology.*

Reid, E. O. F., Qin, J., Chung, W., Xu, J., Zhou, Y., Schumaker, R., et al. (2004). Terrorism knowledge discovery project: A knowledge discovery approach to addressing the threats of terrorism. In H. Chen, R. Moore, D. Zeng and J. Leavitt (Eds.), *Proceedings of the Second Symposium on Intelligence and Security Informatics (ISI'04)* (pp. 125-145). Berlin: Springer.

Riloff, E. (1996). Automatically generating extraction patterns from untagged text. In W. Clancey, D. Weld, H. Shrobe, and T. Senator (Eds.), *Proceedings of the 13th National Conference on Artificial Intelligence (AAAI 96)* (pp. 1044-1049). Menlo Park, CA: AAAI Press.

Ronfeldt, D. and Arquilla, J. (2001). What next for networks and netwars? In J. Arquilla and D. Ronfeldt (Eds.), *Networks and Netwars: The Future of Terror, Crime, and Militancy* (pp. 311-362). Santa Monica, CA: Rand Press.

Rossmo, D. K. (1995). Overview: Multivariate spatial profiles as a tool in crime investigation. In C. R. Block, M. Dabdoub and S. Fregly (Eds), *Crime Analysis Through Computer Mapping* (pp.65-97). Washington, D.C.: Police Executive Research Forum.

Rumelhart, D. E., Hinton, G. E., and Williams, R. J. (1986). Learning internal representations by error propagation. In D. E. Rumelhart and J. L. McLelland (Eds.), *Parallel Distributed Processing: Explorations in the Microstructure of Cognition.* Cambridge, MA: MIT Press.

Ryan, J., M.-J. Lin, et al. (1998). Intrusion detection with neural networks. In M. I. Jordan, M. J. Kearns and S. A. Solla (Eds), *Advances in Neural Information Processing Systems* (pp. 943-949). Cambridge, MA: MIT Press.

Saether, M. and Canter, D. V. (2001). A structural analysis of fraud and armed robbery networks in Norway. In *Proceedings of the 6th International Investigative Psychology Conference,* Liverpool, England.

Sageman, M. (2004). *Understanding Terror Networks.* Philadelphia: University of Pennsylvania Press.

Sarkar, S., and Sriram, R. S. (2001). Bayesian models for early warning of bank failures. *Management Science, 47*(11), 1457-1475.

Schroeder, J., Xu, J., and Chen, H. (2003). CrimeLink Explorer: Using domain knowledge to facilitate automated crime association analysis. In H. Chen, R. Miranda, D. Zeng, C. Demchak, et al. (Eds.), *Proceedings of the First NSF/NIJ Symposium on Intelligence and Security Informatics (ISI'03)* (pp. 168-180). Berlin: Springer.

Schmid, A. and Jongman, A. (1988). *Political Terrorism: A New Guide to Actors, Authors, Concepts, Data Bases, Theories and Literature.* Oxford: North Holland.

Schumacher, B. J. and Leitner, M. (1999). Spatial crime displacement resulting from large-scale urban renewal programs in the city of Baltimore, MD: A GIS modeling approach. In

J. Diaz, R. Tynes, D. Caldwell and J. Ehlen (Eds.), *Proceedings of the 4th International Conference on GeoComputation*.

Schumaker R., and Chen, H. (forthcoming). Leveraging question answer technology to address terrorism inquiry. *Decision Support Systems*.

Schumaker, R. and Chen, H. (forthcoming). Evaluating the efficacy of a terrorism question answer system: The TARA project. *Communications of the ACM*.

Schumaker, R., Ginsburg, M., Chen, H., and Liu, Y. (forthcoming). An evaluation of the chat and knowledge discovery components of a low-level dialog system: The AZ-ALICE Experiment. *Decision Support Systems*.

Shortliffe, E. H. and Blois, M. S. (2000). The computer meets medicine and biology: Emergence of a discipline. In K. J. Hannah and M. J. Ball (Eds.), *Health Informatics* (pp. 1-40). New York: Springer-Verlag.

Silverstein, C., Brin, S., and Motwani, R. (1998). Beyond market baskets: Generalizing association rules to dependence rules. *Data Mining and Knowledge Discovery, 2*, 39-68.

Sparrow, M. K. (1991). The application of network analysis to criminal intelligence: An assessment of the prospects. *Social Networks, 13*, 251-274.

Stamatatos, E., Fakotakis, N., and Kokkinakis, G. (2001). Computer-based authorship attribution without lexical measures. *Computers and the Humanities, 35*(2), (pp. 193-214).

Stolfo, S. J., Hershkop, S., Wang, K., Nimeskern, O., and Hu, C.-W. (2003). Behavior profiling and email. In H. Chen, R. Miranda, D. Zeng, C. Demchak, et al. (Eds.), *Proceedings of the First NSF/NIJ Symposium on Intelligence and Security Informatics (ISI'03)* (pp. 74-90). Berlin: Springer.

Strickland, L. S., Baldwin, D. A., and Justsen, M. (2005) Domestic security surveillance and civil liberties. In B. Cronin (Ed.), *Annual Review of Information Science and Technology (ARIST)*, Volume 39. Medford, New Jersey: Information Today, Inc.

Sun, A., Naing, M.-M., Lim, E.-P., and Lam, W. (2003). Using support vector machines for terrorism information extraction. In H. Chen, R. Miranda, D. Zeng, C. Demchak, et al. (Eds.), *Proceedings of the First NSF/NIJ Symposium on Intelligence and Security Informatics (ISI'03)* (pp. 1-12). Berlin: Springer.

Tolle, K. M. and Chen, H. (2000). Comparing noun phrasing techniques for use with medical digital library tools. *Journal of the American Society for Information Science, 51*(4), 352-370.

Torgerson, W. S. (1952). Multidimensional scaling: Theory and method. *Psychometrika, 17*, 401-419.

Trybula, W. J. (1999). Text mining. In M. E. Williams (Ed.), *Annual Review of Information Science and Technology (ARIST)* (vol. 34, pp. 385-419). Medford, NJ: Information Today, Inc.

Tsfati, Y. and Weimann, G. www.terrorism.com: Terror on the Internet. *Studies in Conflict and Terrorism, 25*, 317-332 (2002).

Tufte, E. (1983). *The visual display of quantitative information*. Cheshire, CT: Graphics Press.

Vapnik, V. (1995). *The nature of statistical learning theory*. New York: Springer-Verlag.

Wallace, R.S. (2004). The Anatomy of A.L.I.C.E. in *A.L.I.C.E. Artificial Intelligence Foundation, Inc*. Available at: http://www.alicebot.org/anatomy.html

Wang, G., Chen, H., and Atabakhsh, H. (2004a). Automatically detecting deceptive criminal identities. *Communications of the ACM, 47*(3), 71-76.

Wang, G., Chen, H., and Atabakhsh, H. (2004). Criminal identity deception and deception detection in law enforcement. *Group Decision and Negotiation*, 13(2), 111-127.

Wang, J.-H., Huang, C.-C., Teng, J.-W., and Chien, L.-F. (2004b). Generating concept hierarchies from text for intelligence analysis. In H. Chen, R. Moore, D. Zeng and J.

Leavitt (Eds.), *Proceedings of the Second Symposium on Intelligence and Security Informatics (ISI'04)* (pp. 100-113). Berlin: Springer.

Wang, J.-H., Lin, B. T., Shieh, C.-C., and Deng, P. S. (2003). Criminal record matching based on the vector space model. In H. Chen, R. Miranda, D. Zeng, C. Demchak, et al. (Eds.), *Proceedings of the First NSF/NIJ Symposium on Intelligence and Security Informatics (ISI'03)* (p. 386). Berlin: Springer.

Wasserman, S. and Faust, K. (1994). *Social network analysis: Methods and applications.* Cambridge: Cambridge University Press.

Weimann, G. (2004). www.terrorism.net: How modern terrorism uses the internet. *Special Report* 116, U.S. Institute of Peace.

Weisburd, D. and McEwen, T. (Eds.). (1997). *Crime mapping and crime prevention.* Monsey, NY: Criminal Justice Press.

Weiss, S. I. and Kulikowski, I. (1991). *Computer systems that learn: Classification and prediction methods from statistics, neural networks, machine learning, and expert systems.* San Francisco, CA: Morgan Kaufmann.

Witten, I. H., Bray, Z., et al. (1999). Using language models for generic entity extraction. In *Proceedings of the ICML Workshop on Text Mining*, Stockholm, Sweden.

Xu, J. and Chen, H. (2003). Untangling criminal networks: A case study. In H. Chen, R. Miranda, D. Zeng, C. Demchak, et al. (Eds.), *Proceedings of the First NSF/NIJ Symposium on Intelligence and Security Informatics (ISI'03)* (pp. 232-248). Berlin: Springer.

Xu, J. and Chen, H. (2004). Fighting organized crimes: Using shortest-path algorithms to identify associations in criminal networks. *Decision Support Systems, 38*(3), 473-488.

Xu, J. and Chen, H. (forthcoming). Criminal network analysis and visualization: A data mining perspective. *Communications of the ACM.*

Xue, Y. and Brown, D. E. (2003). Decision based spatial analysis of crime. In H. Chen, R. Miranda, D. Zeng, C. Demchak, et al. (Eds.), *Proceedings of the First NSF/NIJ Symposium on Intelligence and Security Informatics (ISI'03)* (pp. 153-167). Berlin: Springer.

Yang, Y., Carbonell, J., Brown, R., Pierce, T., Archibald, B. T., and Liu, X. (1999). Learning approaches for detecting and tracking news events. *IEEE Intelligent Systems: Special Issue on Applications of Intelligent Information Retrieval, 14*(4), 32-43.

Zeng, D., Chang, W., Chen, H. (2004). A Comparative analysis of spatio-temporal hotspot analysis techniques in security informatics. In *Proceedings of the 7th IEEE International Conference on Intelligent Transportation Systems (ITSC 2004)*, Washington, DC, October 3-6, 2004.

Zeng, D., Chen, H., Tseng, C., Larson, C., Eidson, M., Gotham, I., et al. (2004). Towards a national infectious disease information infrastructure: A case study in West Nile Virus and Botulism. In *Proceedings of the National Conference on Digital Government Research, (DG.O 2004)*, Seattle, Washington, Digital Government Research Center.

Zeng, D., Chen, H., Tseng, C., Larson, C., Eidson, M., Gotham, I., et al. (2004). West Nile Virus and Botulism portal: A case study in infectious disease informatics. In H. Chen, R. Moore, D. Zeng and J. Leavitt (Eds.), *Proceedings of the Second Symposium on Intelligence and Security Informatics (ISI'04)* (pp. 28-41). Berlin: Springer.

Zeng, D., Chen, H., Daspit, D., Shan, F., Nandiraju, S., Chau, M., et al. (2003). COPLINK Agent: An architecture for information monitoring and sharing in law enforcement. In H. Chen, R. Miranda, D. Zeng, C. Demchak, et al. (Eds.), *Proceedings of the First NSF/NIJ Symposium on Intelligence and Security Informatics (ISI'03)* (pp. 281-295). Berlin: Springer.

Zhang, Z., Salerno, J. J., and Yu, P. S. (2003). Applying data mining in investigating money laundering crimes. In P. M. D. Domingos, C. Faloutsos, T. Senator, and L. Getoor (Eds.), *Proceedings of the 9th ACM SIGKDD International Conference on Knowledge Discovery and Data Mining* (pp. 747-752). New York: Association for Computing Machinery.

Zhao, J. L., Bi, H. H., and Chen, H. (2003). Collaborative workflow management for interagency crime analysis. In H. Chen, R. Miranda, D. Zeng, C. Demchak, et al. (Eds.), *Proceedings of the First NSF/NIJ Symposium on Intelligence and Security Informatics (ISI'03)* (pp. 266-280). Berlin: Springer.

Zheng, R., Li, J., Chen, H., Huang, Z., and Yi, Q. (forthcoming). A Framework of Authorship Identification for Online Messages: Writing Style Features and Classification Techniques, *Journal of the American Society for Information Science and Technology (JASIST)*.

Zheng, R., Qin, Y., Huang, Z., and Chen, H. (2003). Authorship analysis in cybercrime investigation. In H. Chen, R. Miranda, D. Zeng, C. Demchak, et al. (Eds.), *Proceedings of the First NSF/NIJ Symposium on Intelligence and Security Informatics (ISI'03)* (pp.59-73). Berlin: Springer.

SUBJECT INDEX